The Truth Will Set You Free

The Truth Will Set You Free

GROWING UP GAY IN OPUS DEI

TIM POCOCK

Published in Australia and New Zealand in 2025
by Hachette Australia
(an imprint of Hachette Australia Pty Limited)
Gadigal Country, Level 17, 207 Kent Street, Sydney, NSW 2000
www.hachette.com.au

Hachette Australia acknowledges and pays our respects to the past, present and future Traditional Owners and Custodians of Country throughout Australia and recognises the continuation of cultural, spiritual and educational practices of Aboriginal and Torres Strait Islander peoples. Our head office is located on the lands of the Gadigal people of the Eora Nation.

A catalogue record for this book is available from the National Library of Australia

ISBN: 978 0 7336 5253 0 (paperback)

Cover design by Luke Causby / Blue Cork
Front cover photography courtesy of Chris Jon
Back cover photography courtesy of nata_rass / Adobe Stock
Typeset in Sabon LT Std by Kirby Jones
Printed and bound in Australia by McPherson's Printing Group

The paper this book is printed on is certified against the Forest Stewardship Council® Standards. McPherson's Printing Group holds FSC® chain of custody certification SA-COC-005379. FSC® promotes environmentally responsible, socially beneficial and economically viable management of the world's forests.

For the isolated warriors, the brave outcasts, the lone wolves craving freedom. For those trapped by the beliefs of their loved ones, condemned by bias, who dream of a day when they can just be themselves. For anyone who has felt, or still feels, that they are 'less than' simply because they are different from those around them. This is for you.

Contents

Contents

Prologue

Grauman's Chinese Theatre is one of the most iconic Hollywood landmarks of the last century. It played host to thousands of movie premieres from the glory days of Hollywood's golden era to present times and also had a short stint as the home of the Academy Awards in the 1940s. Its courtyard pavement boasts the handprints and autographs of entertainment legends like Judy Garland, Marilyn Monroe, Tom Cruise and Meryl Streep, to name a few. Situated in the heart of Hollywood, directly opposite the Roosevelt Hotel and with the Hollywood Walk of Fame right at its doorstep, the theatre's striking facade is recognisable worldwide, and serves as a shining beacon to young actors and filmmakers who have grown up with stars in their eyes and an ambition to meet their idols at their own level.

I was one of those Hollywood tragics. I had spent years gobbling up everything I could about the movie industry. I watched all the entertainment news shows, constantly read about the latest motion picture announcements and would set my VCR to record every Oscars, Golden Globes and

Emmys presentation. I would buy the DVD and Blu-ray of every film that I loved and watch the behind-the-scenes extras as much as the films themselves. I dared to dream, from my quiet suburban bedroom in the Hills district of Sydney, that I would one day be part of Hollywood's rich tapestry. This is a lofty goal for any actor, and though I never doubted my persistence, there was always a sense that I was shooting too high. I had no connections, no official training and no-one in my life who shared or even understood my dreams. It was, therefore, overwhelmingly surreal to find myself in the back seat of a car driving to Grauman's Chinese Theatre for the Hollywood premiere of a blockbuster action film that I was *actually* in.

It was 28 April 2009 and I was twenty-three years old. Just a few days earlier, I had clocked out of my last ever shift selling movie tickets at a cinema multiplex, where I had worked for five years, packed my bags and headed to Hollywood to see myself on the big screen for the very first time. The premiere was for *X-Men Origins: Wolverine*, a film in which I played a popular superhero called Scott Summers, better known as 'Cyclops'. Yes, the guy who shoots laser beams out of his eyes. *C'est moi.*

It was an out-of-body experience to arrive at the iconic theatre as someone who actually had a right to be there. Stepping out of the car, I immediately became self-conscious about my shoes. In my haste to pack, I hadn't thought about shoes. Apart from family weddings, where I would just pop on my old school shoes for the occasion, I had never been to something so fancy and formal before and had never needed to think about something as mundane as footwear. I had been gifted a bespoke suit from Burberry in Beverly Hills for the premiere, but on the day of the big event, I realised I had never sorted out my shoe situation. In a panic, I threw on a scuffed pair of black-and-white Converse sneakers from General Pants, Castle Towers shopping centre.

As I stepped out of the car, I couldn't help but notice just how much the black-and-white sneakers stood out against the brilliance of the red carpet, and how vividly they clashed with the navy blue of my suit. But I had no time to dwell on that thought. Hundreds of photographers and entertainment news reporters lined the red carpet stretching out before me. Thousands of fans filled the streets, screaming out for a glimpse of their favourite movie stars. I was blinded by the flashing lights and deafened by the screaming crowd. But, without any time to think, I was jostled into position in front of a bank of photographers, each shouting my name so they could get the perfect shot.

As I tried to mask the nervous energy coursing through my veins and pose with the casual nonchalance of a movie star, I was soon whisked away by my publicist once more. Microphones were shoved in my face and, through the haze of the blinding lights, I realised I was being interviewed by the very same entertainment news shows that I had sat at home watching over the past few years. Suddenly I was on the other side of the camera, no longer a mere spectator in the Hollywood machine. As I fluked my way through an interview with *E! News*, Halle Berry walked past me. As I tried to act cool during an interview with *Access Hollywood*, Ryan Reynolds was interviewed directly beside me. And as I stumbled my way through a conversation with CNN, I was upstaged by Mel Gibson and his new girlfriend, who chose that night to make their first appearance at a Hollywood event since the public demise of Mel's marriage. Gasp, scandal!

Halfway through another interview, I found myself being dragged away. My publicist had seen that the main cast, consisting of Ryan, Hugh Jackman, Dominic Monaghan and will.i.am, were assembling for a group photo, and he didn't want me to miss out on that opportunity. I was more or less thrown at will.i.am, who I had never met before, and we all posed like firm friends. I'm a shorter species of human, measuring a staggering 5'8". Fellow cast members Dominic, will.i.am and the film's leading lady, Lynn Collins, were also vertically challenged. Hugh, Ryan and our film's director, Gavin Hood (an Academy Award winner, by the way), towered over us.

'Line up in the order of size,' shouted one of the eager photogs.

'Size of what?' quipped Ryan, in his risqué style that we all know and love.

I took the moment to introduce myself to Will, and he awkwardly introduced me to his fellow Black Eyed Peas band members, though I knew he had absolutely no idea who I was or why I was there. Despite the chaos of that moment, that photo will always be one of my most treasured memories, and I can't help but laugh whenever I see Will and me arm in arm, looking like best buds.

It all happened so fast that I never got a chance to really soak it in. Before I knew it, we were being ushered into the packed theatre. Every one of the several hundred seats were spoken for. As the lights dimmed, I nervously snacked on popcorn from a box that had my own face plastered across it. Before long, there I was projected onto the cinema screen, and the audience erupted in cheers after my first big action sequence. It was a tremendous relief and I'll remember it forever.

After the premiere, as we mingled in the foyer, I was tapped on the shoulder. Anjelica Huston stood behind me. I had shared a scene in the film with her brother, Danny, and she was attending the premiere in support of him. I had never expected to meet someone like her in my life. With her multiple awards and iconic role in the *Addams Family* movies, I had always viewed her as part of the unattainable Hollywood elite.

'You were great,' said Morticia Addams, and I felt like I could die happy.

This was it. This was what dreams were made of. This was the Hollywood fantasy that I had worked tirelessly to achieve.

* * *

However, my feeling of accomplishment that night was overshadowed by a crippling self-doubt. I look back at the photos and cringe-inducing interviews from the red carpet, and all I see is a lost little deer in the headlights. I was a fish out of water and, despite trying to fake it till I made it, I was an impostor. The truth of the matter was, behind the scenes, the Tim Pocock who attended that glitzy event was consumed by a deep self-loathing that had persisted for more than a decade. I had a dark, soul-crushing secret that consumed my every thought and filled me with such profound shame that I hid my true self from literally everyone. I carried the guilt of someone who had committed a heinous crime, like murder, and lived under the constant torment of what my deserved punishment would be. And yet I was no murderer. What I was, in fact, was gay.

Internalised homophobia is a very real and dangerous thing. One of my goals in writing this book is to provide a rare window into the life of someone who struggled with self-hatred during the adolescent years of development in which youngsters begin to flourish, find themselves and start their lives with confidence in who they are and what they can achieve.

The kid who attended that premiere was haunted by the reality of who he was, and the success of that moment wasn't enough to overcome the decades of conditioning and programming that had robbed him of the self-confidence he deserved. The claustrophobic pressures of my religious family, and the constant monitoring and manipulation I faced during my education at the hands of Opus Dei, had left me completely unprepared for the real world, unable to be myself and, most importantly, ashamed of who I was. It would still be a number of years before I would start my journey to find my authentic self and, even then, I would discover that 'coming out' is not as simple as flicking a switch. It didn't all just fall into place, especially because the bubble I grew up in demonised not only homosexuality but also the world at large. It was 'us v. them' in our home – 'us' being devout believers who lived by strict moral virtues and 'them' being the rest of the world, which represented the threat of hedonistic temptation created by Satan. As long as I stayed in that sheltered bubble of pretence, I would be safe. Or so I'd been told. Therefore, the damage that had been done couldn't truly be seen until I started to experience real life. But, like an animal raised in captivity who suddenly finds itself out in the wild, my survival skills just weren't there.

It was like living in pitch darkness my whole life and suddenly finding myself blinded by light. The adjustment period would take time while I continually bashed into walls and tripped over objects in my effort to move forward. And as my eyes slowly got used to the exposure, I was flooded with sensory overload of a world that was completely foreign to me. Unfortunately, any missteps I took ended up as fodder for the captors that held me in my dark cage. It is little wonder that so many people with similar stories didn't make it. I almost didn't.

The following is a deep dive into who I am, what I went through and what I have learned. I am no saint and make no assertions that I have the answers to the problems posed.

I am a deeply flawed, confused, bumbling fool, tripping over my own feet as I explore this thing called life. What I do have are my own experiences and a willingness to share them. For both good and bad, triumph and failure, I have learned a lot so far and, though I would have preferred it differently, I learned most of those lessons the hard way.

There are so many people out there whose experiences are similar to my own. I know that they feel alone, but I am here to tell them that they aren't. There is power in that knowledge.

There are others out there who don't understand that the way they choose to express their beliefs is harmful to their vulnerable queer loved ones who, like I had to, may be hiding themselves as a means of survival. Perhaps this can open some eyes and challenge some hearts.

And there are so many people who are allies without fully understanding the importance of their allyship and the deeper significance of why they are so necessary.

My humiliating plan therefore is to give you a warts-and-all recounting of my life and a thorough examination of the more challenging times. Though I say it with all the love in the world, my overly sheltered upbringing – under the constant spiritual supervision of my mother and the Opus Dei community – played a major part in the challenges I faced and the huge prices that I paid as a consequence.

I therefore humbly submit my story.

CHAPTER ONE

The Grand Times

The first boy I ever had a crush on was an altar boy at St Brigid's Catholic Church, in the idyllic coastal village of Crosshaven in County Cork, Ireland. I would have been no more than seven years old.

Crosshaven was situated on the south-east of the Irish coastline. It consisted of sprawling farmlands atop magnificent cliff faces, a small harbourside city centre that boasted a handful of mom-and-pop shops and white stone cottage-style houses, some with thatched roofing still intact. The streets were narrow, barely paved and rarely able to accommodate two-way travel. They were lined with haphazard dry-stone walls and, every now and then, the crumbling remnants of centuries-old ruins.

My family bounced around quite a bit when I was a child due to the nature of my father's work as a chemical engineer. Though my parents were Australian, I was born in South Africa in the mid-80s, when my parents worked there. I was a toddler when we moved from South Africa to Australia, eventually settling in the Sydney suburb of Concord for a couple of years. I was four when we uprooted again and moved to Ireland.

Crosshaven was a huge contrast to where we had been living in suburban Sydney. For a kid like me with a boundless imagination, it was easy to get lost in the fantasy of such an untouched world with an immense history and seemingly unlimited possibilities. Life there was pure and simple. I loved how quaint everything was in that minuscule town where everyone knew everyone, and you could skip down to the local store, which was run by your close neighbour, who would fill your sweet bag with confectionery for the price of ten pence, roughly twenty cents, and throw in a little extra at no additional cost. I had a good group of close friends and due to the wholesome nature of the place, it wasn't uncommon for us to spend entire days roaming the picturesque countryside without a care in the world.

We lived in a charming white stone cottage called Normandy, situated on Weaver's Point in Crosshaven. It sat at the top of a hill, at the end of an unpaved laneway.

One-car garage.

Fireplace.

Two-bed.

One-bath.

Hot water, occasional.

But it had views to die for.

In front of us, the coastline wrapped around the water, with the Roche's Point Lighthouse directly opposite us, jutting out from a postcard-perfect cliff face with nothing but open ocean beyond. At night, the rotating shaft of light from the lighthouse would sweep at intermittent intervals through the room that my sister and I shared while we shivered in our beds – the radiators lining the walls of our room often unable to produce heat due to our pipes being constantly frozen.

When it was time to bathe, we would have every pot on the hotplates, boiling water to fill our bathtub. And whenever my sister would mysteriously vanish in the evenings, she was sure to be found in the cupboard that housed the hot water unit, which she would be hugging for dear life for the slightest amount of warmth it would give off.

Behind our property lay a potato farm, the owner of which welcomed us to scrounge the dirt for any missed spuds from the harvest. Beside us lay an untamed bramble forest filled with foxes and rabbits, who would eat from the palms of our hands. In the warmer months, if temperatures rose beyond 21 degrees Centigrade, we would get the day off school and splash around in the frigid waters of the local pebble beach. In the winter months, our sloped driveway would ice up just enough for my sister and me to toboggan down it on our oven's baking trays.

On weekends, we would ride horses, visit centuries-old castles in the neighbouring suburbs or drive to the other side of the country for some sightseeing (with me in a sleeping bag in the boot of the car). My sister and I would also frequent a local cow farm, where we encountered our first heartbreak when we connected the dots between the suddenly missing newborn calf we had affectionately named K9 and the veal we had just consumed for dinner.

It's easy to romanticise such an idyllic childhood. But despite the fondness of my memories from that era, it was also the time that I started to become aware that something about me was not quite matching up to what I was meant to be. There was something about the way that I liked looking at that altar boy that didn't align with the world that had been presented to me so far. I had never heard of homosexuality, and the only definition of 'gay' that I knew meant 'happy'. But ours was a very religious and traditional family, and the devout Catholicism that was instilled in me since before my memories began had worked its way into my subconscious without me having the age or discernment to understand them. Ours was a life of strict rules, with very black-and-white definitions of what a proper life should look like.

The driving force behind our religious beliefs had always been my mother. She saw it as her duty to ensure that my sister and I would never set a foot wrong and jeopardise our rightful place in heaven.

***

My earliest memories of Mum are from my time as a toddler in Sydney, in the years before Crosshaven. I remember how much joy and laughter we shared together. Mum was incredibly affectionate, energetic and fun. She only listened to classical music, religious hymns or Gregorian chants, and she would blast them in the house while she cleaned, turning vacuuming into ballroom dancing, and mopping into the

Charleston. I would join in, as toddlers do, picking up the dustpan and broom and trying to mimic her dance moves while most likely making more mess for her to clean. Her nickname for me was George. I've never fully understood why. My favorite teddy bear as a toddler was called George. He was big and had a lot of stuffing around the midsection. Was she trying to tell me something? But as the old saying goes, a boy's best friend is his mother, and this was exactly our dynamic.

Mum was born in 1951 and was the second of nine children. Her family lived in Moss Vale, a small country town in the Southern Highlands of New South Wales. She and her siblings were sent off to boarding school almost as soon as they could talk, even though the boarding schools they attended were within hundreds of metres of their family home. These schools were segregated by gender and their teachers were priests and nuns. They were raised with ideologies that rejected the changes and progress happening in their world, and so by the time they had graduated, they were already decades behind the cultural shifts that had taken place around them. They therefore felt that anyone who had been influenced by the cultural and sexual revolutions of the 1960s and 70s had succumbed to the temptations of Satan, who was obviously using progress as a way to undermine God's vision for the purity of humanity.

This meant that the dating pool was shallow. Mum was therefore only interested in men who held her same beliefs. As such, she, like her sisters, only dated boys from their own sheltered world, most of whom were close friends of my uncles, who attended the male boarding school in their isolated country town. In fact, before Mum married my dad, she had dated another friend of my uncle, who ended up marrying her sister. All of this is to say that at no point was anyone even slightly interested in breaking from tradition. Therefore, their own already-outdated views of the world and constant focus on religious fervour were passed down to future generations.

As a young boy, I had the disciplines of our Catholic faith drilled into my every thought and action, from the moment I woke up in the morning to the moment I was tucked into bed at night. Along with grace before meals, we would start each day with the morning prayer: *O my God, I offer you all the joys and sufferings of this day. Every breath that I should breathe, every movement, every step. Turn them all, dear Jesus, into acts of love that will bring me closer to you. Amen.* We would also attend daily mass, pray the rosary every day and end each night with a deep examination of conscience, in which we were encouraged to think of all the bad things we had done during the day and beg for forgiveness so that our souls would remain pure and acceptable for heaven.

I have vivid memories from this time, prior to our move to Ireland, when we would spend Friday evenings studying catechism at a family friend's house. My parents, sister and I would jump into a van filled with uncles, aunts and cousins and we'd sing *If you're happy and you know it, clap your hands!* while we travelled to a large house filled with other similarly devout Catholic families. All but one of the adults would disappear into a room with a priest for a religious meditation. The remaining adult would usher the dozen or so kids to another room for hours-long lessons on the catechism of the Catholic Church. These were comprehensive dissections of the Ten Commandments and moral teachings from the Bible: lessons for us young folk to carry forward into our lives as children of God. We would learn these lessons off by heart, using rhythm or music for maximum retention, even though we didn't fully understand what we were being taught.

From God's creation of humanity and Eve's sin of eating of the forbidden fruit, we learned that we were all born inherently sinful and needed to apply the rules laid out in the Ten Commandments in order to show gratitude and love for our creator and save our souls from peril. With the story of Cain and Abel, we learned the importance of personal responsibility and the cost of sin, while simultaneously being warned of the dangers of jealousy and envy. Through the story of doubting Thomas – one of Jesus' disciples who hadn't been present when the resurrected Christ appeared before the rest, and therefore questioned the legitimacy of this apparition – we learned never to question what we were being taught about our religion, as this was a sign of shameful weakness and a lack of faith.

For my young mind, these lessons were already putting up barriers in my ability to think for myself. They made an enemy of my instincts and impulses, and ultimately resulted in a coercively controlled dependency on the Catholic faith and the adults teaching it to me. This meant that when the Ten Commandments were broken down into hundreds of sub-commandments that each of the ten represented, life became about strict obedience, with the threat of hell constantly at the front of my mind.

If we ever rebelled against any of these teachings, retribution would be swift and severe. And any act of disobedience would always be linked to our betrayal of God. Something as simple as not brushing my teeth within seconds of being told to do so would be defined as breaking the fourth commandment, 'Honour thy father and thy mother', and so I wasn't just being a kid not wanting to go to bed yet but a sinner at risk of going to hell. On such occasions, my father's belt would be used against my backside as an earthly reminder of the punishments that awaited me after death if I continued down this path. The second commandment, 'Thou shalt not take the name of the Lord thy God in vain', was defined as any unacceptable language, which was subjectively up to the parents themselves to decide. Any swear words or foul language, which in our household included the terms 'shut up' and even 'I'm bored', were therefore deeply sinful. Our extended family believed strongly that children shouldn't be in the household during the daytime and, as such, we were constantly locked outdoors. If we dared to admit 'I'm bored', we would be dragged by the ear to the laundry room and forced to eat soap to cleanse our mouths of the sinful words we had uttered. And I have a foundational memory of witnessing the discipline one of my aunts used on a cousin when he had disobeyed her instruction. He was struck in the face, resulting in him falling down a flight of stairs. He was left with a bloody nose and no dinner as chastisement.

These punishments weren't a regular occurrence. I don't want people to think that I was being physically abused and beaten around the clock. Ours was a very loving home. But when punishments did happen, they were extreme. They drove the point home that disobedience was met with potent consequences that were only a shadow of the punishments of hell. On the flip side, however, there was never an earthly equivalent that recognised obedient behaviour. That was reserved for our heavenly afterlife and required patience for our eventual death.

I was at most four years old when these ideas were being ingrained into my brain. And with only my family and their like-minded community as my guides, it was of the utmost importance that my future life would emulate their strict, conservative values as closely as possible. But obviously I was far too young to grasp the full significance of what I was learning, especially the part about marriage being strictly between a man and a woman ...

***

Our strict daily religious practices didn't wane when we left Sydney, but the seismic shift in our lives when we moved to Ireland resulted in a change in Mum. Not only were my sister and I both school-aged by then, so we weren't in the house as often, but she was also unable to get an Irish visa that would allow her to work. Mum was a teacher, and she had no fulfilment in her life without teaching. She had never wanted to be a housewife, especially in a country where she didn't have family or friends she could fill her time with. She started to volunteer at a youth shelter for the homeless, providing education and support. She also started to visit the elderly in our small country town, giving them company and assistance. Though these things did take up some of her time, and as silly as it sounds to say that a five-year-old could recognise this in his mother, it was like a light had gone from her eyes. She wasn't the same bundle of energy anymore. But it is admirable that with the time she did have on her hands, she spent it in service of others. She really was a beautifully intentioned person.

When it came to things that she did want, however, she took them to the extreme. This started out fairly simply. We would visit Blarney Castle at least once every couple of months. It dates as far back as 1200 AD and has quite a storied history. Atop a tall tower of the castle is the Blarney Stone. Folklore dictates that anyone who kisses the Blarney Stone will be bestowed 'The Gift of the Gab'. From reading this, you can probably tell that I have kissed it many a time. After ascending a long, winding and increasingly narrowing staircase, you come out to a high rooftop. The Blarney Stone itself is on a wall of the turret, positioned over a gap in the floor, with a flimsy grate placed over the twenty-five-metre drop below. To kiss the Blarney Stone, you lean backward over the drop and give that mouldy old chunk of rock a quick peck. As a teeny-tiny five/six/seven-year-old, I took great pride in being braver than the adult tourists who would freak out at the challenge.

The grounds of Blarney Castle had mysterious caves, witches' gardens and other crumbling relics from centuries ago. My sister and I loved to spend our time exploring the fantasy world that it provided. However, it was always clear that our intention in going there was never for the castle grounds itself.

Adjacent to Blarney was a large wool mill, and *that* was Mum's playground. Mum rarely joined us at the castle, as she preferred to spend her time at the wool mill. Once we joined her, we would spend longer in that sea of sheep fur than we would at the castle. Though their inventory rarely changed, we would spend hours trying on jumpers and turtlenecks, and Mum would agonise for lengthy periods of time while choosing between two almost identical garments. But it was understood by us that this was *Mum's time.*

However, as the months progressed, *Mum's time* morphed to completely focus on our religion. Without students to teach, our home became her classroom. She felt the need to continue the spiritual development we had received in Australia. On the weekends, we would drive to Cork for Sunday mass at the cathedral even though the local Crosshaven Catholic church was just a few minutes from our home. There were always people on the front steps of the cathedral begging for money from the faithful.

Mum would promise them cash as long as they came to mass and sat in the pew with us. After mass, and having paid off our new 'converts', we would then spend hours at a Catholic library in Cork.

Mum was constantly on the lookout for new material to absorb in order to continue her spiritual growth. Aside from the armful of books she would walk out with, she would borrow recorded lectures from bishops around the world and make the whole family listen to them. We would go on road trips around Ireland and have lectures by Archbishop Fulton J Sheen blasting over the car stereo. Sheen was born in the nineteenth century and had written more than seventy books. He had spent an extensive amount of time on radio and television during the 1950s and was seen, with the exception of the Pope, as the world's leading voice on Catholicism. And so it was paramount that she shared his teachings with us, even though the majority of his content was from forty years prior. Another of her favourite recordings, that we spent hours listening to in the car, was a series of lectures about hell – with graphic depictions of the horrors that awaited sinful souls, based on firsthand accounts from various saints throughout history who had supposedly been gifted with visions of hell by God.

As the car drove through the Irish countryside, I would huddle in my sleeping bag in the boot, terrified by what I was hearing: the weightless souls of the damned being tossed around in the burning pit of flames, the never-ending shrieks of agony, the animal-like demonic creatures, the absence of any hope and the eternity of it all. You know, just some casual light listening for a six-year-old.

When Catholic conferences took place in Ireland, we would drive for hours so she could attend. Dad, my sister and I would sit in the car for an entire day in a parking lot and wait. I vividly remember one occasion when the conference centre was adjacent to a water park. She had sold my sister and me on the promise that we would be hurtling down water slides and having the time of our lives. However, when we arrived, the water park was shut for the season and, once again, the three of us just sat in a car for hours while she attended the lectures.

Mum also kept up a rigorous correspondence with her siblings and a priest in Sydney who gave her spiritual direction. Most memories I have of being at our home in Ireland revolve around my sister and me playing outside while Mum was writing her letters. Always writing her letters. She had eight siblings, so it was a lot of work. The correspondence grew more frequent as time went on. Whenever she sent a letter to one of her sisters, she would ask my sister and me to record ourselves on a cassette, giving updates to our cousins. As the frequency of these correspondences increased, my sister and I started to run out of things to say. We were six and ten, respectively, schoolkids living in a very small country town. Not a whole lot was going on in our lives. Except when we finally got a colour TV, and my mind was absolutely blown by the fact that the Smurfs were actually blue. Who knew?

As Mum's isolation grew, so too did her need to shelter us from outside influences. This meant that even something as mundane as entertainment, for my sister and me, was intensely monitored. We weren't allowed to listen to popular music from the time, as it contained language and ideas that Mum didn't approve of. We weren't allowed to watch the television shows and movies that other kids were consuming. This was the era of *The Simpsons*, *Teenage Mutant Ninja Turtles*, *Captain Planet* and *My Girl* – all of which were strictly off limits. The kids in *The Simpsons* and the teenagers in *Ninja Turtles* were bratty, outspoken and rebellious. *Captain Planet* promoted an adoration for the earth and was therefore blasphemous to the one true God. And *My Girl* showed two teenagers kissing, which was obviously highly immoral. That *Smurfs* viewing was therefore a once-off.

I have a memory of a friend's birthday party during that time. When the birthday shenanigans were over and the sugar coma started to kick in, the exhausted kids slumped in the living room in front of *The Simpsons* while waiting for their parents to collect them. My mum showed up to get me and found me watching the show with the rest of the kids. I was absolutely lambasted on the way home for being so disrespectful of her wishes by participating in the viewing rather than helping the mother clean up. I was six.

Another time, a friend from school whose birthday, like mine, was at the end of October had asked if we could have a joint Halloween-themed birthday party. Mum viewed Halloween as a demonic ritual that glorified the occult and was a mockery to our Catholic faith. Therefore, I was not allowed to share that kid's birthday party or attend it, and because all the other kids were going to his party, I just didn't have one.

The entertainment that my sister and I *were* allowed to consume was films from decades earlier. It was the early nineties and yet the few films we had on rotation included *Mary Poppins* (1964), *The Sound of Music* (1965), *My Fair Lady* (1964), *The King and I* (1956) and *The Wizard of Oz* (1939), which better represented the wholesome values that our family wanted to instil in us. When my friends and I would get together to play, I would struggle to connect with them about the pop culture crazes of the day. To me, the Teenage Mutant Ninja Turtles were just a bunch of buff turtles who shared names with prolific artists from hundreds of years ago for some reason. The Simpsons were yellow just because, and Bart and Lisa were brats who didn't represent how children should behave. At my young age, I had to justify why I was so out of the loop by parroting my mum's views and doubling down on judgement about things I honestly knew nothing about – simply because I had been told to. It strikes me that perhaps it is this same childish mentality that has influenced so many people to judge something like homosexuality for no other reason than the fact that they simply don't understand it, but have been told to be against it. But perhaps I'm getting ahead of myself.

Modern fashion, too, was something that we were kept away from. This was the age of the one-tone matchy-matchy tracksuit, and bowl cuts were all the rage. And while I agree, looking back, that these were definitely regrettable sartorial missteps, I'm not convinced that my turtleneck sweaters, lime-green corduroy pants and Cary Grant hairdo were screaming high fashion, either.

I have another memory from that time: when my sister and her friends dressed me in one of her frocks, put a bow in my hair and, with childlike exuberance, tried to pass me off to my parents as being their new female friend. This only resulted in another lecture, and was the first time I heard the term 'cross-dressing'. Mum, as you might have guessed, was against this. She was livid that I had dressed like a girl, and used Michael Jackson as an example – he was far too effeminate, with his high cheekbones and girly hair, to be an accepted form of male. And it was made clear that any man who dresses as a girl is an insult to God's design.

At the end of the day, it seemed that anything modern was the enemy. The changes that were taking place in the nineties were a threat to the kind of life that my parents wanted for us, and they felt that exposure to anything current or new would corrupt us. Mum would tell us that these things were 'of this world', and that we must reject the devil's temptations to try and lure us into being 'worldly' people. Instead, our focus should be on the *next* world by putting into practice our faith and emulating the examples of our parents, aunts, uncles and the other faithful followers we had grown up with. The pressure to never deviate from the hardline, black-and-white definitions of who I should be, how I should behave and how I should ultimately turn out was already sitting firmly on my shoulders. If something seemed different from what I was told was acceptable, it had to be wrong.

* * *

This brings me back to the altar boy. I didn't really know why I liked the look of him; I just did. He also went to the same school as me. It was a small school in a small town, with only sixty or so students from kindergarten to Year 6 and school grounds that could easily fit into a motel car park. Recess and lunch breaks were additional chances to see *him*, and my eagle eyes would scan the playground for him the moment the bell rang for break. And, though my fascination was completely innocent, it felt like something that had to be kept secret. This *was* different from what I had been told was acceptable, so it had to be wrong. And the hellish visions from my mother's lectures rang loudly in my ears.

It never amounted to anything other than a childish curiosity, as we left Ireland abruptly a few months after my seventh birthday. So if he was my first crush, I can confidently say that I can pinpoint the genesis of my limp-wristed, swaying-hipped, homo-lisped fagness to around seven years of age. Obviously, at the time, I had absolutely no idea how to interpret the 'crush' feels. All I knew was that I liked looking at him. I liked his face. I thought his clothes were cool, and that he looked good in them.

People have questioned me about this memory, saying that it would be far too young for me to have understood my sexuality. And yet I would challenge that by saying that most straight people are never tasked with identifying when they first could acknowledge an innocent attraction. For them, being straight was normal, so they never needed to pay attention to any burgeoning feelings they may have had when they were younger. And yet they're partially right. I didn't recognise this as being a sexual preference at all; how could I? Sexuality had not yet manifested itself in me. But since when does an instinctual attraction mean sexual desire? It was merely the dawning of a realisation that I wouldn't understand for some years to come.

It struck me that I was looking at him the way that Maria looked at Captain von Trapp in *The Sound of Music*, the way that Miss Anna looked at King Mongkut in *The King and I*. As these films were my only real reference point outside of the life that my family had presented, along with the Catholic teachings I was receiving, attraction and romance could only ever exist between a man and a woman. Having said that, I had always found myself siding with the female heroines of these films. Though these movies were approved by my family as non-corrupting entertainment, I couldn't help but be swept away by the total smoke show that Christopher Plummer was as Captain von Trapp, and watching Yul Brynner prance around shirtless in *The King and I* also caused a stirring of something within me. The point is, I began to realise that the way I looked at the altar boy was the way that boys were meant to look at girls.

So did that mean that I wasn't ... normal? And if I wasn't, there was no chance I would alert anyone to that fact. Something about me was actively working against my goal of eternal life with God, and that something, whatever it was, had to be kept secret.

Ultimately, however, none of this was preoccupying me at the time. It was merely something that I clocked about myself while being thoroughly distracted by the idyllic life we were living in our gorgeous, untouched part of the world. The innocence of my attraction to that altar boy was matched by the innocence of life in general. And before it had a chance to evolve into something more worrisome, we left, and I never saw him again.

CHAPTER TWO

The Butterfly Effect

It was Christmas, 1992. As the Irish weather grew steadily colder, snow and sleet started to fall, coating our front lawn in a glistening white carpet. The school term ended and my sister and I had a two-week holiday break to celebrate the festive season. It was our third Christmas away from our parents' families in Australia, and Mum decided we would take the opportunity to make a quick ten-day trip to Sydney to bask in the sunshine and enjoy a good old-fashioned Aussie Christmas with the relatives we had sorely missed over the past few years. Dad was unable to get time off work, and though it was sad that we would be leaving him alone during such a family-oriented time, the rest of us were excited for another round-the-world adventure. I remember sitting on the plane with my sister, practising clichéd Australian phrases with glee. We had both developed thick Irish accents at this point, so I'm sure we provided endless entertainment for the other passengers while we loudly rehearsed how to say 'g'day, mate' as convincingly as possible.

Our excitement was short-lived, however, as this trip turned into a nightmare almost as soon as it had begun. We flew to Sydney via Los Angeles. Mum had assumed that, as we had a connecting flight, we wouldn't need to clear US immigration, but she was wrong. Therefore, we were travelling without US visas. When we got to the customs desk at LAX, we were arrested. My mum, sister and I were held in a jail cell for several hours while we waited for our flight from LA to Sydney. Eventually we were escorted onto the plane by the police and started our second leg of the trip. Unbeknownst to anyone, I had contracted chickenpox, and the symptoms started to show themselves during the fourteen-hour flight to Sydney. I developed a fever and projectile-vomited all over our seats, causing chaos for the cabin crew, not to mention the poor unsuspecting victim in the remaining seat on our row, whose tray table was now decorated with chunks of chicken, carrot and peas. The perfume that the cabin crew doused our row in didn't improve matters. To this day, I shudder whenever I get a whiff of a fragrance even remotely similar and haven't been able to stomach chicken fricassee ever since.

When we landed in Sydney the drama continued, as we were held at customs for hours because my sister had packed a pair of boots she had recently worn on farmland in Ireland, and the crusted mud on the boots posed a threat to the fragile Australian ecosystem. My mum would have been in her early forties at the time, with two young children in her care, and I can't imagine the levels of stress she was under during this ordeal.

Irony has quite the sense of humour. We had made this trip in order to spend time with our family. However, due to the highly contagious nature of chickenpox, I spent that Christmas day sequestered in my grandparents' bedroom while dozens of aunts, uncles and cousins celebrated the merriment of Christmas lunch downstairs. This did little to stop the spread, though, as I had already passed it on to my sister, and soon several of my cousins fell victim to the same fate. But something else eclipsed all of that. Not long after the debris of torn wrapping paper had been cleaned up and the leftovers from the sumptuous Christmas roast had been devoured, Mum informed us that her father had cancer and, as such, she had made the decision that we wouldn't be returning to Ireland. We were to remain in Australia, indefinitely.

I have always viewed this decision as one of the most pivotal moments in my life. Though it might sound dramatic, our unscheduled return to Australia was the start of the bad times. There is, however, an equal argument to be made that staying in Ireland may not have afforded the same opportunities in life that ended up leading me to the career that I feel so much fulfilment from, which makes this a real sliding doors moment that often leaves me wondering *what if?*

But one thing I do know for sure is that this decision set in motion a series of events that eventually led to me being enrolled in a school called Redfield College and introducing me to the world of a secretive sect within the Catholic Church called Opus Dei. I would spend the next ten years there as a pupil in what can only be described as complete misery.

Dad was unable to just abandon his job and our home in Ireland, and so my grandparents took Mum, my sister and me into their lavish home with open arms. With its giant crystal chandelier in the entrance hallway illuminating the grand spiral staircase to the upstairs living quarters, it was a significant upgrade from our humble Crosshaven cottage, and my sister and I no longer had to share a room. But I mourned the loss of my friends, who I had never said goodbye to. I missed my dad, and the tight-knit family unit that I had been so used to. And I was shocked to discover that, though I thought of Mum as a strict religious disciplinarian, she paled in comparison to her father.

Doc, as my grandfather was affectionately known, was a World War II veteran. He had been a navigator for a Lancaster bomber that had taken part in many raids, and he lived with an immense religious guilt for the part he may have played in the deaths resulting from missions. His days were planned with militaristic precision, which suddenly became our norm. His prayer life made my mum's look weak; where she would sometimes show leniency in skipping a daily rosary from time to time, this was non-negotiable for him, and his unshakable opinions on appropriate ways for children to behave meant that there was an entirely new set of strict rules for us to learn and follow. But despite always feeling like I needed to walk on eggshells, I also felt tremendous affection for him. He had a great sense of humour and would take pains to distract my sister and me from the increasingly emotional phone calls that Mum would make to Dad, who would take six months to join us in Australia.

My grandmother, too, was an endless source of entertainment. An immaculately stylish woman, Granny dressed like the Queen of England, with a matching hairstyle that was teased to within an inch of its life. Despite her elegance, she was a cheeky woman who had a thirst for sports cars and treated the roads of Sydney like a NASCAR racecourse. They were both incredibly generous to us and did so much to make up for the turbulent time we were going through.

I was soon enrolled in a local Catholic school and started to make some new friends. Meanwhile, Mum secured a teaching job at the same school my sister had started attending: Tangara School for Girls. Tangara and its brother school, Redfield College, were relatively new institutions that had been set up in the late eighties by an organisation called Pared, a term that stands for 'Parents for Education'. The founding families were people that my parents had grown up and gone to school with themselves. They rejected the modernisation of the Catholic school system and wanted to have more control over the curriculum being taught to their kids. These schools were therefore based on the principles of Opus Dei and followed the directives of its founder, Josemaría Escrivá. Though known for its secrecy, it is considered even by most practising Catholics as extremely conservative in its ideals and teachings.

Though Mum was not an actual member of Opus Dei herself, the values that it represented were exactly in line with what she wanted for us as kids. She had been reluctant to send me to the Catholic school I was attending. She didn't like that it was co-educational, because she believed that boys and girls were far too distracting for each other and should be separated, and she viewed the school itself as being too 'trendy' (modern) in its teachings. When the 'Healthy Harold' education van would make its visits to the school, I wasn't allowed to attend as, though it promoted health and wellbeing for children, it did also touch on educating the kids about their developing bodies and paved the way for sex education, which Mum vehemently opposed. And so, after just two terms at that school, I was removed. Mum pulled some strings with Pared and managed to get me placed in Redfield College midway through second grade. The school I had been going to was about to do its yearly 'debut' of new students, which included a dance between the boys and the girls. We had been rehearsing it for a few weeks and then, all of a sudden, 'Nope', and I was removed. It was another upheaval, another loss of new friendships, and I felt constantly buffeted around like a human pinball hurtling one way only to be suddenly sent rocketing off in a different direction.

Thankfully, my dad was finally able to leave Ireland and join us in Australia.

However, our family dynamic had definitely shifted. My parents didn't show the same closeness and affection for each other that I had witnessed before all this happened, and seven-year-old me understood why. Though I understood my mum's decision, I resented that these changes had thrown all our lives into such chaos, and that we were uprooting our lives for her. We soon moved to our own place in the Hills District of Sydney to be closer to the schools she approved of, but at least some sense of normality was finally restored. However, as I would find out, Redfield College would end up being the worst change of them all.

CHAPTER THREE

The Work

The Redfield College website does mention that the inspiration behind the school is Opus Dei and its founder, Josemaría Escrivá – though it takes some digging to get to that point. It states that the school chaplains are Opus Dei, but that 'in all other aspects, the schools are the responsibilities of the Board of Pared or their own administrations'.

It should be pointed out that many members of the Pared Foundation board, as well as the administrators of the schools, are members of Opus Dei or, at the very least, strong conservative supporters of that community, like my mother. So I do think it is quite misleading to suggest that Opus Dei's connection with the schools is merely through their chaplains.

As a student there from age seven to eighteen, I can tell you categorically that Opus Dei's influence on these schools was all-encompassing.

Opus Dei translates to 'Work of God' and is referred to by its members as 'The Work'. Members of Opus Dei mostly fit into one of two categories: numeraries and supernumeraries.

Opus Dei numeraries are men and women who take a vow of celibacy and devote much of their lives to the organisation, although they are neither priests nor nuns. They sometimes adopt methods of religious corporal punishment, like sleeping on wooden boards and wearing barbed metal thigh belts, called cilices, to cause irritation – all discomforts that they offer up in sacrifice to God.

They have daily tasks set for them, which they are obligated to follow. These would include their daily mass and prayers schedule, proselytising (which essentially means converting non-believers) and acts of charity. These tasks would then be shared with their Opus Dei chaplains, and additional strategies are put in place in order for them to be more successful in their duties. Their wages are made available to Opus Dei, and an allowance is provided to them for essentials. In many cases, they live communally in university or school 'study centres' that are run by Opus Dei, such as Warrane College and Creston College, which are single-sex boarding facilities at the University of New South Wales, and Nairana and Eremeran in the Hills District, which are after-school study centres affiliated with Redfield and Tangara.

Supernumeraries are members of Opus Dei who still dedicate their lives to the directives of Escrivá but do so as non-celibate members. Their vocation is to be parents, and to bring into this world more children who uphold the values and teachings of Opus Dei. The rest are known as cooperative members, meaning that they aren't actual members of Opus Dei but still subscribe to their ideals and methodologies and, as such, attend spiritual formation sessions known as 'circles'. My parents would often attend these circles, Mum more so than Dad. These were regular gatherings that were usually held at one of the study centres affiliated with the schools. Men and women would attend separate circles, which would mostly be conducted by an Opus Dei priest and would involve prayer, guidance and spiritual direction in how to foster the teachings of Opus Dei in their everyday lives – at work, at home, as spouses and as parents.

Several of the teachers at Redfield were Opus Dei numeraries, including the principal. It was the same at Tangara. There were also a number of teachers who were supernumeraries, some of whom were parents, uncles, aunts, cousins and family friends of the students. The core group of parents and teachers that established these schools was from a generation that had all attended school together and been raised with archaic ideals, even for their own time. This made the Pared and Opus Dei community incredibly insular and almost impossible to endure if you weren't part of their clique.

I started at Redfield College shortly before my eighth birthday. It was my third school since I had turned seven. After all the disruption of the past year, and as a naturally shy kid, I found it very confronting to be starting all over again ... again.

I remember my first day at Redfield vividly. Mum was running late for her own schoolteaching duties, so she dropped me out the front and told me to find someone to tell me where to go. It was a cold day. Dark clouds hung overhead, with a constant drizzle spitting down as I trudged through the puddles, surrounded by complete strangers and without a clue of where to go or who to speak to. I will go so far as to say that I consider the gloom of that day, how lost I was and how I didn't have anyone to turn to for help, as a metaphor for my entire time at that school.

The school buildings were decidedly pink. Local rival schools knew us as 'Pinkfield', though the chairperson of Pared would always describe the colour as 'Peach 101' at our yearly prize ceremony. The entrance to the school was grand and austere, with a sloping driveway framed by pillared gates that overlooked the multiple sports fields, land for future developments, a large dam featuring a statue of Our Lady, tennis and basketball courts, and behind those, a number of demountable structures, which would be my first classrooms as a student.

I struggled to make friends, which hadn't been an issue in my past schools. I had become quite introverted and had lost my will to really connect with the other kids. How was I to know whether we would vanish off to Sweden or Argentina in another six months and start all over again ... again ... again? I had lost my belief that it was worthwhile investing in friendships, and my young self reacted to all these changes by becoming withdrawn and even more shy.

But what made it harder was the insulated nature of the Pared/Opus Dei world. Though the school grounds were large and impressive, the school itself was very much in its infancy. With an average of twenty students per grade, a generous estimate of the total school population would be around 200 students from Years 2 to 12. There was a cluster of six or so main family groups within the Pared community who, for the most part, had decades of friendship between them. They had introduced their siblings, cousins and family friends to the schools. These were families with large headcounts, some having a dozen or more children spread throughout the school's grades. So at least fifty per cent of the school was populated by family members of the people running the place. Many of them were also employed as educators. It therefore didn't feel as much like joining a school as it felt like marrying into a large family who were all a bit *iffy* about you. I was also sporting a very thick Irish accent that immediately identified me as different and made me feel like an outsider from the get-go. After a few months of merely coexisting as a pupil there, I did eventually find a few friends, most of whom were outsiders like me who didn't have a plethora of siblings, cousins and best friends in this tight-knit community. So, for the first couple of years, it was tolerable.

The religious education was constant, from the start of the school day till its end. But this didn't strike me as any different from how my own family had always operated. We would begin each school day by lining up on the basketball court in military formation in our class grades. A teacher on a megaphone would shout out militaristic instructions, 'At ease!' and 'Attention', which we would follow over and over until the megaphone decided that we were all following along dutifully. We would then recite a morning prayer. This would often be in Spanish, like other prayers we would repeat throughout the school day, as Spain was the birthplace of Opus Dei. Mass was offered daily and each grade would attend once a week, with students free to be present more often if they wished. Confession was part of our religion periods, with each child being sent off one by one to make their reconciliation. The Opus Dei chaplain would know which class group was coming for confession and, even though we'd be sitting behind the privacy screen, he would spend the time trying to glean information so that he could identify us.

'Bless me, Father, for I have sinned. It has been one week since my last confession.'

'Very good, very good,' the priest would reply. 'Go on.'

'I was disobedient to my mum when she asked me to take the garbage out, so my dad had to take it.'

'Ah, I see. Sometimes we can be selfish, but we must always be mindful of others. What do your parents do for work?'

'Dad's an engineer and Mum's a schoolteacher.'

'Oh? Where does she teach?' he would probe.

'Tangara,' I would reply reluctantly.

'Excellent. She must be a good woman. What else?'

'I threw a hairbrush at my sister during a fight.'

'Does she go to Tangara too?'

'Yes, Father.'

'Is your sister older or younger than you?'

'Um ... she's in Year 8.'

'Is this Tim?'

Pause. Sigh. 'Yes, Father.'

With the illusion of anonymity provided by the privacy screen now shattered, the priest would then be able to refer to our past conversations and confessions and provide me with spiritual direction that was bespoke to my own journey. As a younger child, I found it embarrassing enough when my gravest sin was a typical sibling fight, but as I grew older and the sinfulness of masturbation was being drummed into me constantly at school, in church and at home, you can imagine how awkward it was to have to admit something like that, only for the priest to then address me by name when condemning the immorality of lust.

Most subjects were taught through the lens of Catholicism. For example, when the history curriculum topic was King Henry VIII, we focused more on St Thomas More, the Catholic advisor to King Henry who opposed his divorce and was made a martyr due to the courage of his convictions. Much like the Opus Dei numerary teachers who would wear the cilice, St Thomas More was famous for wearing a hairshirt that irritated the skin as a form of corporal punishment. He was also rumoured to have used 'the discipline', a whip used by the devout faithful on themselves in order to offer up their suffering to the glorification of God. Many people associate the discipline with Opus Dei, as it was made famous in Dan Brown's *The Da Vinci Code* – Silas, the villain of the book, is a monk in the order of Opus Dei who violently whips himself before a crucifixion statue while repenting for his sins. I hate to disappoint, but there are no self-whipping monks in my story, nor did I ever see any evidence that the discipline was in use among the Opus Dei members surrounding me (when asked about it, our numerary teachers would shut up like clams and place us in immediate detention). But I do think it is quite telling that instead of really studying King Henry VIII and his actual legacy in the history of the world at large, we were studying a different man whose level of faith matched that of the numeraries we were being taught by, and that behind the smokescreen of history class, we were being taught to never question the interpreted rules and regulations of our religious teachings.

When it came to other subjects, we were often simply not taught certain things. We would collect our textbooks from the school before the start of the new year and, on a number of occasions, certain parts of the textbooks had been removed or blacked out. The school would not only refuse to teach the content, but also didn't want us to be reading it in our free time – subject matter like evolution and reproduction, for example. The school leaders, as well as my family and anyone I knew, believed in intelligent design and, therefore, it would be a waste of time to fill our heads with the nonsense of evolution. God created us exactly as we are, and so the notion of evolution was preposterous and degrading to humanity. And when it came to reproduction, sex education was simply never taught. Sex was seen as the ultimate temptation for a person and was to be avoided at all costs. Its purpose was solely to create a deeper union between the couple through sanctified Catholic marriage, and to conceive more children of God. The less us kids knew about it, the better. I never had the 'birds and bees' chat with my parents. I knew absolutely nothing about it. And school wasn't informing me, either. So for me, at least, sex education was never addressed. I simply had no idea about any of it. I honestly thought that sex happened through the bellybutton, and that a woman gave birth from there. Umbilical cords were attached there, so it made sense to my childish, uneducated mind. I'm not being hyperbolic; that was literally how I thought it all worked.

When I was in Year 10, our class sat the School Certificate examinations. The science paper contained a section relating to sex education. The principal of our school, a celibate Opus Dei numerary, came into our classroom ahead of this and explained to us that the sex education portion of the paper was only 5 per cent of the full exam, and therefore if we got everything else right, we would still be able to achieve 95 per cent. He did, however, graciously encourage us to answer any of the questions in that section, should we know them. One question was a cross-section diagram of the female reproductive system, asking us to list the various parts. I had heard of something called a 'Filipino tube', so I confidently labelled everything with that, thinking I was sure to at least get one point for it.

This was only shortly after I had discovered that females didn't, in fact, have penises. As I had never been taught a thing on that subject and was a gay kid with no interest in the naked female form, I had simply never thought about it and assumed that everyone had a penis because that's how you pee. One day, when one of my aunts had a newborn daughter, I was watching her bathe the infant and suddenly thought, *But where's her thingemy?*

I'm not trying to be vulgar with that admission, but just want to point out the level of naivety and ignorance that resulted from being *that* sheltered. My personal view is that it is irresponsible and potentially harmful to shield kids from learning healthy sexual standards. Not only did this result in pregnancies outside of marriage, but for the queer kids, it provided no responsible forms of sexual health education that would go a long way in ensuring their safety when they finally ventured out into the real world. Similarly, AIDS was only ever portrayed to me, at home as well as at school, as 'the gay disease' – God's punishment for homosexuality.

I remember studying disease during science period one day, and AIDS was being discussed. I would have been around fourteen at the time and had been terrified about my dark secret for years already. With so little understanding of the things being taught, I was afraid that maybe gay people were born with AIDS, which could mean I had it. So I raised my hand and asked the teacher how gay people got AIDS.

'Use your imagination, Mr Pocock,' replied the teacher, before sending me to the principal's office and putting me in detention.

I was a scared kid, genuinely petrified that I had been born with a terminal illness that I didn't want, as much as I didn't want to be gay in the first place.

This kind of reaction from a teacher wasn't uncommon at Redfield, though. Many teachers seemed to have anger management issues. My Year 7 class teacher was notorious for blowing up, going from zero to a hundred in the blink of an eye. His face would turn puce as he yelled derogatory insults to the student or class. It went far beyond a teacher disciplining his students for being disruptive. And yet this was a man who we were meant to be holding in high esteem as a devout Opus Dei supernumerary – and therefore someone to aspire to be like. I remember another occasion with our sports teacher, who, upon discovering that the sport shed padlock had been broken, decided it was our class that had done it and launched into a fifteen-minute verbal tirade that culminated in him calling us all 'gutless turds' and putting the entire class in lunchtime detention. And if any student dared to ask a numerary teacher about the corporal punishment that was involved in their daily vocation, the teacher would get immediately defensive. They wouldn't give straight answers, as Opus Dei was always shrouded in secrecy, and even if the kid had been deliberately facetious in asking the question, the punishment always outweighed the crime. We all learned pretty quickly to never provoke a teacher before recess or lunch break because, if we did, we would simply not be allowed out of the classroom after the period ended. Instead, we would spend the breaks with our foreheads against our desks and our hands on our heads. Another teacher decided he had the authority to hold us back in class even after the school day was finished. For an hour he kept our class locked in the classroom, with each of us missing our buses or car rides home. Eventually, the mother of one kid came down to the classroom and yelled at him about his abuse of power. We all sat in awe as she took him to task. When she was done, he clasped his hands in prayer and simply walked away, leaving us teenagers to figure out how we would all be getting home that day.

On the other hand, many of the numerary teachers were focused on developing friendship bonds with the students. This was especially the case for the younger teachers. They wanted to come across as *cool* to the kids so that they could connect with them on their level. There were whispers that some of the younger numerary teachers would buy cigarettes for their teenage students and turn a blind eye when they smoked in the out-of-bounds areas, which I witnessed on a daily basis. At its most innocent level, this could be attributed to the fact that these numerary teachers had never really developed beyond teenage years themselves due to taking their vow of celibacy so young, thus keeping them in a state of somewhat suspended animation as they grew older, resulting in them never really leaving the high school environment and only wanting to make connections with other people who shared their maturity level. But, more cynically, this could be seen as a tactic used to ingratiate themselves with vulnerable teens in order to recruit them into their own way of life. For us students, it was like walking a tightrope never knowing what you were going to get – a teacher who wanted to be your best friend or one who would fly off the handle at a moment's notice.

One of the unique selling points of the school is what it currently calls its 'Mentoring System'. Back in my day, however, this was called their 'Tutorial System'. As I am sticking to my own experiences, that is how I will refer to it. Each student at the school was assigned a 'tutor' who was a member of the teaching staff. With the exception of a small few, these 'tutors' were predominantly Opus Dei numeraries or supernumeraries. Every few weeks, at random unannounced moments, our assigned 'tutor' would knock on the classroom door and extract their 'tutee' from class. If it was my turn, I would then have a twenty-minute discussion about my life while walking the school grounds. While a small portion of this time would be spent talking about my education, my 'tutor' and I mostly conversed about my spiritual growth as a child of God. Over the course of ten years at the school, my 'tutor' changed several times, which was common. They focused on my spiritual development, and they would give me advice on how best to form as a follower of our Catholic faith, as seen through the eyes of Opus Dei. Each term, my assigned tutor would report to our Opus Dei school principal, who would then have a meeting with my parents to discuss how I was forming as young man, which would influence how my parents approached their responsibilities in continuing to shape me at home.

In addition to this, the school provided a study centre called Nairana. Boys from the high school grades were encouraged to attend Nairana after school hours, and the school's bulletin, *The Weekly Red*, would advertise their services and activities. We would catch the bus to Pennant Hills train station after school, stop off at the shops to buy chips and soft drink, and then walk up the hill to the study centre. It was, in fact, a residential house in a residential neighbourhood, and the home of some of our Opus Dei numerary teachers and our school chaplain. There would often be visiting numeraries from Spain, who would reside there as well. It had a large study room, with dozens of cubicles where we could do our homework. During these study sessions, much like with the 'tutor' at school, I'd occasionally be tapped on the shoulder by one of the numeraries there, and we'd go for a walk around the block to talk further about my spiritual life. *Had I started to notice girls yet? What did I think of girls? Why didn't I think I had connected with the other boys? Did I need further spiritual guidance? Had I ever thought about joining Opus Dei and becoming a numerary?* You know, because most teenage boys are dreaming of a life of celibacy.

After ninety minutes or so of homework, we would enter the house's small chapel, where the priest would give us moral teachings for forty-five minutes, and then we'd spill outside and do boy stuff, like sports. They had weekend activities and school holiday camps as well, all under the supervision of the Opus Dei members who ran the place, most of whom were our teachers. And all these activities were advertised and encouraged by the school.

All of this is merely to point out that the school and Opus Dei were more or less one and the same, with their reach extending into the family home, which was part of the school's design. Students were completely immersed in their world, unable to escape. For some, this posed no issue. With supernumerary parents and numerary siblings, and with their own interests and ideals matching up with how that world worked, it was a perfect and affirming experience for some. But people like myself are evidence that this one-size-fits-all approach to our education and growth as young men did not actually work. As I was a 'different' kid, their attempts to mould me in their image only felt like manipulation. And, as a 'different' kid who had also started to notice other boys at school in the same way that I had noticed that altar boy in Ireland, I finally started to understand the ramifications of my innocent attractions. I liked boys the way I was *meant* to like girls. Others started to notice it too, and it was obvious that the world I was living in would never accept that.

So let me paint a picture of what it was like for a kid like me to grow up in that world, with its rigid beliefs and the structure of constant surveillance between school and home. I'm brought back to the memory of seeing Redfield's school motto for the first time, emblazoned on its school crest.

Veritas Liberabit Vos.

The truth will set you free.

As the years went on, this motto rang more and more false to me. Not just because of the secrecy behind the tactics used to manipulate the students, but because it became ironically clear that there was no freedom in *my* truth – only condemnation. With no escape from the unwavering opinions and vested interests of everyone who had control over my life, my developing and unchangeable homosexuality made my time in their virtuous Catholic world a living hell.

CHAPTER FOUR

The Cage

The homophobic bullying that I experienced at Redfield College started when I was nine years old. This wasn't due to any actual homosexual act that I had committed, but was derived solely from the heteronormative definitions of 'male' and 'female' that this schooling community held dear. Certain interests and behaviours identified a masculine man, and I didn't live up to them. A couple of years into my time at the school, my musical abilities somewhat accidentally led to a career as a musical theatre and opera performer. And while these activities made me feel alive and free and fulfilled, they immediately made me a target in that world, as these weren't 'masculine' behaviours. And so this passion and talent of mine started to make my life a whole lot worse.

I was in the third grade at school when a chance opportunity led me to join the Australian Youth Choir. The choir was scouting schools in the area and paid a visit to Redfield. The representatives walked around the room while each class sang the national anthem, and if they heard a promising voice, they slipped a piece of paper into the student's hand, offering an official audition. I didn't sing. The choir representatives asked me if I was too shy to sing, but I replied in my thick Irish accent, 'I just moved here, I don't know the national anthem.' So I ended up singing 'Twinkle, Twinkle, Little Star' solo, and they handed me an offer to audition. I had played piano since I was three years old and, by this time, had already started to excel through the grades. Redfield's music offering at the time was very sparse. The school had a brass band, led by another parent of multiple students. I played the trumpet in the band, though our prowess was not something to brag about. As a subject, music wasn't taken very seriously. At best, the students felt ambivalence toward it, while most considered it 'fruity'.

I had a deep love of classical music. While my mum enjoyed listening to it, no-one else in the family showed any skill or passion for it. I craved an outlet for my musical interests, and it was clear that I wouldn't get that from school or at home.

I was allowed to audition for the choir and was successful. The choir gave me the opportunity to not only develop my musicality, but also share my passion with similar kids. After some months of singing with them, performing at big venues and even recording an album with Australian music veteran Darryl Cotton, I was encouraged by the choir director to audition for a local production of *The Sound of Music* – a film that I was deeply familiar with, as you know. At only nine, I had never considered the idea of being a performer or actor. And yet, after a few years of turbulent change, something about this opportunity spoke to me. It just felt right. I was desperate to be involved, and begged my parents to let me try out. Thinking back on that audition, I had never doubted that I would be cast. I remember singing on stage in front of the judging panel then sitting on the floor in the auditorium foyer, surrounded by hundreds of other hopefuls waiting for the results, and never once doubting that the role was mine. Oh, how I wish I could feel the same way in my auditions these days!

I was cast as Kurt von Trapp. Though it was an entirely new experience for me, the theatre world just made sense and I adapted to it immediately. It was a life-changing moment and I felt truly connected to who I was as a person. I discovered how I thrived in rehearsals, how deeply the music and story affected me, and I had never felt more alive. It was this experience that first made me feel like I had an idea about how I wanted my future to look.

I came alive on stage. The shy kid who never felt like he fit in suddenly felt at home, and my confidence grew with each performance.

Then, one evening, as I was exiting the stage door after a show, I was approached by an audience member who, to my amazement, was affiliated with the Australian Opera Company. They expressed interest in me auditioning for the upcoming opera season at the Sydney Opera House.

I was ten when, only a few months later, I first set foot on the Sydney Opera House stage. The suggestion by the Opera scout had led to me being cast in a lead role in Opera Australia's 1996 season of Mozart's *The Magic Flute*.

It was a huge privilege to learn and perform music written by revered historical composers, guided by the greatest musical minds Australia had to offer. The rehearsal process was exhilarating. Though it tapped deeply into my love of classical music, it developed my abilities as an actor as well. When we finally put it all together with the orchestra, costumes and lavish sets, I was overwhelmed by the scale and sheer spectacle of it all.

The curtain rose on opening night of *The Magic Flute* and a beast was born. I had a rush of excitement and adrenaline when performing on one of the most recognisable stages in the world before thousands of people each night. Over the next five years, the Sydney Opera House became my home. At the end of each opera season, I was always invited back and ended up in twelve productions with them over the years. I spent a couple of those years performing simultaneously in two operas per season, and I lived for every minute of it. I might have been young, but it felt like what I was *meant* to be doing. It felt natural.

However, this thing that I loved so much ended up becoming the source of my torment at Redfield College.

To the kids at school, being an opera singer was 'gay'. Singing, full stop, was not a masculine activity. To take it on professionally was the ultimate extreme. And so the bullying began. Though I hadn't been overly popular, I hadn't been universally disliked until that point. The name-calling had mostly stuck to innuendos about the last four letters of my surname, C-O-C-K (of which I've heard every iteration and am positive that no new ones could exist), and barbs about my lack of prowess in sports, which was seen as a must for the boys. Mum had tried to get me into rugby, her favourite sport and something to which the men in her family had an ardent devotion. I found rugby hideous. I'd spend most of the games face down in the mud being stampeded by studded boots. I didn't see the point in simply throwing a ball around in order to touch it to the ground at the end of the field. Maybe it was fun for some, but it wasn't for me. Mum tried cricket next. I came back from my first cricket practice with a black eye because I'd misjudged a catch, so that was out too. After that it was soccer. I wasn't terrible, so I kept it up for a bit, but it felt like something I was doing just to prove that I could do 'boy' things. I could think of more pleasant ways to spend those Thursday evenings on the practice pitch, or those Saturday mornings in matches against other schools. However, as my opera career started to take off, I stopped playing altogether as I didn't want to risk injuring myself and being unable to perform. I chose the 'girly' thing to do.

This made me an easy target. The success I was achieving at that young age was made a mockery of and the kids at school were relentless. I was viewed by the other students as inferior and weak. Meanwhile, the kids I was performing with on stage accepted me for who I was. They made me feel that my uniqueness was what made me valuable.

It was a very confusing and difficult time. By day, I was being constantly harassed and abused. I was called 'faggot', 'poofter', 'homo', 'gaylord', 'butt pirate', 'procock', 'poofcock' and any other derivative you can think of. But by night, I was receiving standing ovations from thousands of strangers who appreciated the centuries-old art form we were performing. At school, the name-calling soon transitioned into physical abuse. Pokes turned into shoves. Shoves turned into punches. And punches turned into kicks.

One day, while minding my own business eating my lunch, I was pushed down a steep hill by a group of five classmates, who then crowded around and kicked me in the face and body until a teacher pulled them off me. No punishment was given to these kids. Most of them belonged to influential founding families of the school, and one in particular came from a family that had been a significant financial donor. When punishment had been threatened, this boy's father called Mum at home and threatened to remove his funding if his child faced any repercussions. Mum had taught his daughter in primary school, and had since been made the principal of the primary school at Tangara. Not wanting to cause a stir with her benefactors, she chose the schools over me and I felt very betrayed when she showed where her loyalties lay.

Without the fear of discipline, the students had a free pass to continue their abuse. I had my belongings stolen and often thrown into the toilets. I was singled out during PE classes, which would usually be a game of footy. I would find myself tackled to the ground even though we were playing touch. The teacher would simply blow his whistle, turning a blind eye to their behaviour. I therefore became *that* kid who always had an excuse not to participate in the game, regularly 'forgetting' my sports uniform, which only reinforced their opinions of me. And when I did take part, I was the kid who was always chosen last, with the opposing team jeering at the bad luck of the team that was stuck with me.

This belittling wasn't only reserved for break times or group sport activities, however. It continued during class, with whispered insults and objects being hurled at me. The teachers knew what was going on, but as many of the perpetrators were their relatives, in-laws or even children, the most they were reprimanded was by being told to be quiet.

Initially I reported the bullying, but that only made things worse. At best, my complaints would fall on deaf ears, but if action was taken and the students were spoken to, it would only be a matter of time before they exacted their revenge on the playground. As I walked through the school halls between classes, the kids would start chanting my surname. They would swarm like a pack of hungry hyenas until one of them initiated an attack. I would be intentionally tripped over, have my workbooks knocked out of my hands and shoved down stairs. Spat on, punched from behind or crowded around while torments were shouted at me by kids of all grades.

And yet, by night, thousands of people were paying to see me perform, surrounded by other artists who encouraged what I did and had similar interests. I was popular among the other opera kids I performed with. I had made friends so easily and never felt like I had to keep looking over my shoulder. I didn't care that I was being paid; that wasn't why I was doing it. I genuinely loved it. I came alive on stage. And I was good at it. It was like I was living a shadow life during the day and was being brought back to life at night. My true identity only existed on the stage.

For most of this period in my school life, my appointed 'tutor', or 'mentor', was the school vice principal. He was a supernumerary. As these tutorial sessions were meant to be an opportunity to express ourselves and seek guidance, I would talk about how miserable life at school was becoming. Rather than acknowledging the targeted abuse and using his position to combat bullying of this nature, his emphasis was always on how I was the common denominator in the issues, and that I needed to look inward in order to understand why other people didn't like me. *I was the problem.* Over the years, I could sense his boredom with my recurring issues. He would often call me a 'broken record' and his advice was always the same: I needed to stop making myself such a target. I told him that I wasn't. Why would I seek out this constant harassment? I just wanted it to stop. He told me I needed to develop similar interests to the other boys and make more of an effort to connect with them. There was never any discussion about how the other kids should be less judgemental of someone who had different interests to *them*. Where was *their* advice to develop similar interests to *me*? And why should we all be interested in the same things in order to get along? Since when was being somewhat different something that should be highlighted and abused?

Whenever I posed these arguments to my tutor, he would always deflect, and on one occasion told me that I was too 'anal retentive'. I didn't understand what that meant. At the time, all I thought was that his use of the word 'anal' didn't feel like an appropriate thing to say to a child. But as an adult, looking back, I see a man making efforts to divert the conversation out of territory he wasn't comfortable with.

I was also constantly bringing things up to my parents, in the hopes that they would save me from what had become an unbearable situation. However, as the school's tutorial system was built around working in tandem with the parents, everything I had discussed with my 'tutor' was already being passed on to them, along with advice from the school about how to address it. Therefore, I was hearing the same advice and direction at home. The influence of the school and its teachings obviously went far beyond the school walls, and as a teenager, I was helpless against the interference that the school had in my home life. With Mum's role as a primary school principal within the same hierarchical structure of the Pared school system, and having become a 'tutor' at her own school herself, she not only placed a lot of value on the directions given by my own 'tutor' but also didn't want to rock the boat within the organisation that paid her bills and was her entire social sphere. Whenever I cried to her about how I was being made to feel, she would refer to scripture and suggest that, like Jesus, I should 'turn the other cheek' – a biblical lesson that encourages the faithful not to retaliate in the face of hatred, but rather to welcome the persecution as suffering that can be offered up to God for our own salvation. She spun it as a 'blessing' that would bring me closer to God. She also told me that I could afford to 'butch up a bit' and would constantly comment on my swaying hips when I walked, or the limpness of my wrists.

'You look like a sissy boy,' she would often say. She would slap my wrists if she felt like they were too limp, or comment, 'Don't walk like that, people will think you're too girly.'

I soon learned that there wasn't much point in trying to stick up for myself. No matter how much I brought it up, or who I brought it up to, the answer was always the same. *I was the problem*, and *I* needed to change.

The thing is, I didn't *want* to change. I liked what I was good at, and I enjoyed what I was doing with every fibre of my being. A thrill of excitement would flow through me at the commencement of any new opera season, and I had no greater joy in life than heading to the Opera Centre in Surry Hills for rehearsals. The first few weeks were strictly for singing rehearsals and learning the music and lyrics in their languages of origin: French, German, Spanish and Italian. In these sessions, we were also taught the translations so that we knew what we were singing about. Next, we would be introduced to our director and creative team and spend several weeks plotting out our movements on stage and perfecting them. After that, we would gather with the entire cast and the full orchestra for what is called a sitzprobe, a rehearsal where the true brilliance of all the musical elements come together with the orchestra. And the next step would be rehearsing on the actual Opera House stage, in full wardrobe and make-up, with our full set, lighting and sound, in order to iron out the final kinks. After a final dress rehearsal, we would be ready to go. The entire process took months and required a focus and dedication far beyond what the other twelve-year-old kids at school were capable of, but also gave me a much-needed break from the people who made me feel like my only significance was how disliked I was.

Bubbling under the surface, however, was the torment inside my head. As I grew older, I had come to realise that I *was* exactly what I was being accused of. Gay. Though able to appreciate female beauty, I simply wasn't interested in looking at girls the same way that I liked looking at boys. Some of the students at my school – and dare I say it, even some teachers – were incredibly handsome. I would furtively look at them when I could, wishing that I didn't find them attractive but unable to deny that I did. When Mum watched the rugby, with all those well-built men running around in tight-fitting shirts and short shorts, or when we watched Olympic swimming featuring lean, muscular men with very little clothing on, I wasn't exactly watching for the plot. When Mum, my sister and I watched the classic BBC adaptation of *Pride and Prejudice*, featuring a devastatingly handsome Colin Firth, I found myself swooning over Mr Darcy just as much as they did, though I also thought Bingley was exceptionally cute as well. While my sister was able to vocalise her appreciation for these men, I had to keep my thoughts to myself. That rite of passage was denied to a guy like me. I had to pretend instead that the women in that show were gorgeous. I even had a crush on one of my opera co-stars, Teddy Tahu Rhodes, whose gorgeous baritone voice was matched by his good looks and cut-marble physique.

It was undeniable that the innocent attraction I had noticed for the altar boy in Ireland had now, as a hormonal teenager, transformed into something sexual. I could no longer hide from myself that the way I was *supposed* to feel about women was how I felt about men.

However, within my family, my school and my parish church, the only messaging about homosexuality was that it was a mortal sin. An abomination. Something that was diametrically opposed to God's will and could only result in eternity spent in hell along with serial killers, rapists and Hitler. Whenever gay rights were brought up in the political world, our family would pray that the so-called 'gay agenda' wouldn't succeed. The gay rights movement was seen as the devil's work, corrupting the purity of God's creation. Whenever the annual Sydney Gay and Lesbian Mardi Gras took place, Mum would refer to it as a modern-day Sodom and Gomorrah, and we even sometimes spent the night of Mardi Gras at our local Catholic parish for an all-night vigil to pray for the sinful souls taking part. Whenever pop culture promoted gay characters through music, film and TV, words like 'disgusting', 'vile' and 'blasphemous' were used to describe them. And when the judgemental bubble that I lived in gossiped about a child within our community who had 'turned out gay', questions about their upbringing were raised, along with negative opinions about where their parents had failed them. I felt the pressure of not forcing my family into that same conversation.

There was another student at my school, a grade or two above me, who had a beautiful singing voice. He, too, had spent a brief period singing with Opera Australia, though only on a couple of occasions. Suddenly, he disappeared from my school and was sent off to a Catholic boarding school in the country. He ended up taking his own life.

I attended his funeral. On the way home after, I remember my mother commenting on how sad it was for the boy's mother to know that her son's soul was now in hell. Whether the whispered gossip about his sexuality was true or not, suicide was also a mortal sin, for which hell was the only outcome. My mother's sympathy came across to me as a patronising pity.

Other kids at my school who were similarly targeted for their suspected homosexuality were sent off to religious camps so that they could correct their course. One or two of them were brave enough to admit their sexuality and consequently suffered even more than I did. As a witness to all that while still in the early stages of development myself, I could not see how honesty was the best policy. So I kept it to myself, and I berated myself for this unchangeable thing that I couldn't control. I cried myself to sleep at night, praying with complete sincerity that I would wake up in the morning and no longer be gay. When that didn't work, I prayed that I would wake up as a different person. There were boys at my school who were popular, and handsome, and confident and loved for who they were. I wanted to be them, even for just a day. I wished I could walk down the school halls and be appreciated rather than targeted. I wished I didn't have to live in fear of each school day. I wished to no longer be me.

But, at the same time, this broke my heart. In spite of everything, I liked the abilities I had and the joy I felt while performing. I was sad to think that, if I did wake up as another person, the things that I held dear to my individuality, like my sensitivity and my musical ability, would no longer be part of who I was. But the shame and guilt that I felt about my evil secret were stronger. I was terrified of hell. The descriptions of hell I had grown up with reverberated inside my head. At night, when the lights were off and I was trying to sleep, I would sense the presence of Satan in the darkened corners of my room and cling onto my rosary beads. I also had a small statue of Our Lady and a crucifix on a chain around my neck, which I clutched to my chest while I prayed the 'Our Father', 'Hail Mary' and 'Glory Be' on repeat until I eventually fell asleep. I was so scared and ashamed of myself that I didn't want Tim Pocock to exist anymore. Without fully understanding it, I was suicidal. And I wasn't even fifteen yet.

The teachers at school continued to brush aside my complaints. My parents were also ignoring the suffering I was going through and, soon, puberty started to take its course. I began to notice that my arms were getting hairier and I knew that this was a sign that my voice would change. In my naive understanding of how puberty worked, I stole my dad's razor and shaved my arms and legs, thinking that this would stave off the inevitable. I was desperate to cling onto the one thing that gave me purpose, fulfilment and escape in life. However, the inevitable happened. My arms kept getting hairy no matter how often I shaved them, and I was struggling more and more to hit the high notes. My opera career would soon be over, the friends I had made there would soon be just a distant memory, and the fantasy world that saved me from my daily anguish would be gone forever.

My last opera was Baz Luhrmann's *A Midsummer Night's Dream*. It was a beautiful production. The stage was a whimsical three-level tree house with a lake underneath that magically reflected the fairy lights hung above. I played one of the fairy children – or 'gopies', as we called them. My costume was an Aladdin vest over pink chiffon with beaded pants. My skin was painted pink and I was adorned with a bejewelled pink skullcap. We threw our audience headfirst into Shakespeare's world from the moment they set foot in the theatre. I absolutely adored that production. But I also knew it would be my last.

One of the other saving graces of the opera was that I would spend a couple of weeks away from school during the intense weeks of rehearsals leading up to opening night. As both my parents worked and couldn't take me to and from rehearsals, I would spend those weeks living with my grandparents so that my grandmother could be my chauffeur.

I was already close with my grandparents, but spending so much time with them during those days brought us even closer. My grandfather was very proud of my singing and would refer to himself as my 'manager'. He had been battling cancer for years at this point and, despite his frailty, still got up every morning to squeeze fresh orange juice for my grandmother and bring her breakfast in bed. We would go to church every morning and stay for about an hour afterward to pray. He knew his time was almost up and spent every waking moment in prayer.

While I was in rehearsals for *A Midsummer Night's Dream*, his health took a turn for the worse. I decided to record a CD of twelve tracks and gave it to him with a card saying, 'For my manager'.

Despite his health issues, my grandmother still took me to my rehearsals every day, and we'd pray the rosary for him in the car. I was once again feeling a dread in my stomach that things were about to change drastically. My grandfather's impending death seemed to mirror the upcoming end to my opera career. My voice would change, I would no longer be able to escape to my grandparents' house for weeks at a time and avoid the torture of school, and I was about to have my first real encounter with death.

As I left the Sydney Opera House after my final performance of *A Midsummer Night's Deam*, I remember looking down from the Harbour Bridge at the iconic Opera House sails glistening in the waters, and weeping silently about what I knew I was leaving behind for good. I didn't make my emotion visible to my parents in the car because there was no point in expressing myself to them. And besides, crying wasn't a manly thing to do. I wasn't just coming down from the high that each production had given me over the years; I was also scared about how I was going to survive school now that my lifeline had been taken from me.

My grandfather passed away a couple of weeks afterward. The last time I ever sang as a boy soprano was at his funeral. The decision was made that my grandmother would come and live with our family. To accommodate her, we needed to move to a much bigger place. And so, just a few short weeks after the final chapter on my opera life, we moved. My grandmother was now part of our household, two of my cousins moved in with us, and my sister, who was twenty years old, got married and moved out. Another seismic shift, with the only constant being my misery at school.

I started to beg my parents to let me leave Redfield. Surely my years as a professional performer, along with the dozens of awards I had won over the years in eisteddfods for my piano and singing, would qualify me for some of the performing arts schools in Sydney. I knew so many kids from those schools, co-stars from my various operas, who didn't seem to suffer at school like I did. Moreover, I had more than proven myself for that kind of education. Redfield's music offering was minimal at best, they didn't offer drama as a subject and also had years' worth of history representing nothing more than misery for me.

I ended up successfully applying for the Sydney Conservatorium of Music High School and another performing arts school, receiving an offer for a partial scholarship at both. I attended orientation days at each school. It was a new experience to be in a school environment without constantly looking over my shoulder. The kids at these schools had similar interests to me as well as performance experience, and the things that made me a target at Redfield made me popular among them.

I was desperate to escape and begged my parents to allow me to leave. However, after many lengthy conversations and consultations with my teachers at Redfield, Mum told me, 'The most important thing is your religious education.' And with that, my parents withdrew my applications to those schools. I was to remain at Redfield. I had no say in the matter. My complaints, my ability, my achievements meant nothing. I had nothing left to bargain with. I learned that I had no power. I had no voice. I just had to accept the decisions that were being made for me. So I shut up like a clam.

It was impossible to repair the damage already done between me and the rest of the school. With my voice falling on deaf ears and my years of proven ability meaning nothing more than a temporary phase, the only option was for me to lie low and keep myself out of harm's way. Though I was no longer on the payroll of Opera Australia, the verbal, physical and psychological torments from the Catholic school I was forced to remain in stayed the same, if not worsened. No longer able to get through the days by looking forward to a rehearsal or performance, I had to find other ways of coping in that inhospitable world. And I did this by hiding. At recess and lunch, I would eat my food in a toilet cubicle. I stopped contributing to classes, opting instead to put my head down, do the work and get out of there. Even at home, I retreated into my bedroom, locked the door and shut everyone else out. At least when I was alone, I was safe.

The hardest part of it all was that I was facing this torture on the mere suspicion that I was gay. No-one knew for certain except me. How much worse would it be if they knew that they were actually correct? Ironically, one of the reasons why I had been changed over to Redfield was my Mum's firm belief that boys and girls would pose too much of a distraction for each other during the adolescent years of growth. However, I was constantly distracted from my education, not just by the never-ending fear I felt every day, but because, as a gay kid at an all-boys school, I was surrounded by temptation every day. It was a sin to even think lustful thoughts, and yet my eyes would fall onto one of my boy crushes in the distance and butterflies would fill my stomach. More often than not, my crushes were also kids who picked on me.

It's such a shame that attraction and abuse got so muddled up together at such a young and impressionable age. I always wished I could have had a healthier way of understanding my sexuality. I wished I could express myself as freely as my sister and female cousins did, with their infatuations with movie stars and music icons. They had photos of them in their bedrooms and were free to openly discuss which Backstreet Boy was the cutest, or debate between Brad Pitt and Matt Damon.

I had some definitive opinions of my own about these matters, and yet had to keep them to myself. As small as that might sound, it is an innocent and healthy rite of passage for teenagers who are starting to understand their own heterosexuality, and a freedom that is taken for granted. My own sexuality had to remain packed away, repressed and resented. If it was a matter of choice, I would have chosen to be straight. I wanted that with all my soul. Being gay was only causing pain – not because of the so-called sin that it represented, but because of the harsh opinions of God's righteous followers who I was surrounded by. Who in their right mind would *choose* to be gay in that environment?

I developed insomnia, lying in bed begging God to give me the choice to be straight. I had been taught that 'faith could move mountains' if it was sincere enough, and I couldn't have been more sincere in my wish to actually exercise *choice* over this matter. But God never changed me. So I would drag myself out of bed after another sleepless night and turn up to school the next morning, still the same old Tim, ignoring the name-calling and dodging the spitballs and punches, all the while shooting surreptitious glances at the cute boy down the hall. As I left for the school day my parents would flippantly say, 'Have a good day,' and I stopped replying, 'I will.' Instead, all I could muster was, 'I'll try.'

Despite my best efforts to be as invisible at school as I could be, it was impossible to escape ridicule. Eventually, the boys realised I was eating in the toilets. They'd dip toilet paper into the toilet bowls and hurl it over the cubicle partition.

On one occasion, one of them managed to lift the door off its hinges, and I was plucked out and thrown into the urinal trough. One of my classmates – the son of a teacher at the school, mind you – threw me through a plate-glass window. Though I was relatively unharmed, the real rub was that he somehow manipulated me into taking the blame for it.

My breaking point came during a school camp in Year 10 that took place at a former boarding school in the Southern Highlands. One of my main bullies emptied my suitcase out of the second-storey window, with all my clothes landing in wet mud below. Though other kids had been standing around and egging him on, it was fascinating to see how quiet they all became when I snapped. I chased him through the dormitory with murder in my eyes. He flung open the fire escape door and started hurtling down the metal stairway. Next to the door was a large floor broom. I picked it up. It was sturdy and heavy. I threw it at him. It hit him square in the back of the head while he was halfway down the staircase. He crumpled and fell down the remaining metal stairs. As he was taken away to get stitches, I was sternly rebuked for my behaviour. I had gone too far, and I was punished. Incidentally, he was the same kid whose dad had threatened to cut off financial support for the schools when he had beaten me up several years earlier. And now, all these years later, he was getting stitches in hospital and I was a 'violent maniac'.

Added scrutiny was placed on me as a consequence. My school 'tutor' started to see me more regularly, and he and my parents decided that I should spend more time at the school's study centre, Nairana. Students begin attending Nairana in Year 7, right around when puberty starts. This coincided with a shift in our religion classes at school to a focus on purity education. Masturbation causes blindness. Masturbation causes infertility. Masturbation is a sinful act in defiance of God's intentions for reproduction. It was a sin to even have a thought that could lead to arousal. The priest in confession would blatantly ask, 'Do you touch yourself sometimes?'

I think it was no coincidence that when students were at this age, the school started encouraging us to spend our afternoons, weekends and school holidays at the study centre with a group of celibate teachers. After establishing a bond with the students, the teachers would subtly start encouraging the teenagers to think about joining Opus Dei. Looking back now, it feels so much like grooming.

I hadn't gone to the study centre as often while I was performing, due to my schedule. But now I had all the time in the world to go, and it was what I was explicitly told to do.

I could think of nothing worse than becoming even more immersed in that world. To me, this would only result in further exposure to the very same people who were harming me in the first place. However, I wasn't given the choice. The numeraries who operated the study centre were the same teachers at school who spent their time trying to befriend the students. As they wanted to remain popular with the kids, and I was the oddball of the group, they were more interested in joining in on the ostracism rather than stamping it out. A couple of them openly disliked me, which resulted in a meeting being called with my parents where a teacher freely admitted that he didn't like me and had intentionally picked on me in class. The upshot of this was that there was no protection provided during the hours spent at the study centre. In fact, it was worse, because these men weren't acting in their capacity as teachers on school grounds anymore, so their responsibility was lessened.

The feeling of being constantly watched was now unmistakable. It felt like they wanted to stamp out my individuality so that I could be rebuilt in the way that they wanted. With my 'tutor' giving me frequent spiritual advice, the school chaplain figuring out who I was during confession, another numerary taking me for further spiritual direction at the study centre, and my parents supporting and promoting every piece of advice that came from this surveillance, it was impossible to escape the feeling that I was being strategically manipulated by all the people around me to become someone I wasn't. It felt like a concentrated effort by a group of people who all agreed that there was something wrong about me that needed fixing. I felt like a captured animal backed into the corner of a cage.

This just caused me to retreat further and further into myself and I developed major social anxiety. It got to the point that if I heard a person laugh from 100 metres away, I would naturally assume they were laughing at me. I second-guessed everything I said and the way I said it, how I walked, how I stood, how I sat. The hypervigilance I developed was exhausting but, at the same time, I had to pretend that nothing was wrong. Internally I was screaming out for help, but asking for it in real life had proven fruitless. So I stayed quiet, spent as much time as possible by myself, away from any potential judgemental eyes, and I just waited out the term of my prison sentence. Within a couple of years, I would graduate, and then I'd be free.

The only saving grace in the last few years of my education at Redfield came in the form of my English teacher. As clichéd as it is to say, I had found my equivalent of Mr Keating of *Dead Poets Society* fame. He recognised my strengths and abilities and encouraged them. He was the only person at school who I felt really understood who I was and what I was capable of and, in those last two years at school when all hope felt lost, his belief in me got me through. He nurtured my love of the arts, and constantly inspired me with his recommendations of films to watch and directors to study. He went above and beyond to ensure that he educated me in my passions. On the days I knew I had classes with him, I would actually be excited to go to school.

Thankfully, the last year of school was so busy with examination preparation that I was mostly spared the torments that had characterised my time at Redfield. There was still a complete lack of respect from the younger students, who had witnessed me being targeted by their older siblings and were now taking their own shots. One or two minor physical altercations took place, but I was fairly numb to it all at that point.

But there was one thing that did sting. A yearly tradition at Redfield was to have a caricature drawn of the graduating class. An artist from the Year 11 class would be commissioned, a theme would be picked, and each student would be depicted according to that theme. My year's graduation caricature theme was a zoo, with each student represented as a different animal. I was depicted as a pink butterfly. The artist who did it was the son of one of the schoolteachers, who was a supernumerary. He made it clear to me while he was constructing the work that he was making me a pink 'fairy' because I was gay. After years of slurs and abuse, the school more than knew what was going on, and yet the artwork was approved and hung on the walls. To this day, the mockery of my sexuality, and a symbol of the school's response – or lack thereof – to homophobic bullying, is immortalised in the hallways for all to see.

I think the most striking thing about my time at Redfield was how hypocritical that world was. While declaring itself to be a shining example of devout Catholicism, the school I witnessed and experienced was at odds with this. One of the main mantras recited over and over again by our priests, teachers and parents was that 'God is love', and it was our duty as Catholics to try and be as godlike as possible. To me, that meant showing love to everyone we encountered, and in everything we did. And yet the verbal and physical abuse that I went through, the archaic, judgemental beliefs and manipulation by the secretive organisation I was surrounded by, didn't feel like love at all. Rather, they felt like targeted coercion, based on judgement, that were designed to hold me back from being myself, and from discovering the real world outside of their organisation – which, by extension, prevented me from ever being honest and authentic about my true self.

I am convinced that there was a genuine concern among the school community, and my parents in particular, that I *was* actually gay and that I needed this manipulation in order to be saved. It is no secret that the numeraries kept lists of the students who they were 'working on', and I definitely felt like I was a target. It was clear that my resoluteness in never folding to their ways influenced how the numerary teaching staff educated me, and led them to turn a blind eye to the persecution I was facing. At least two boys from my class had taken their vow of celibacy and became Opus Dei numeraries when they were still teenage students. In my opinion, these practices rob children of their agency. Without ever truly being given the opportunity to discover who they really were and how they actually fit into the world, they had already made a life commitment based solely on the constant bombardment of Opus Dei's ideologies.

I think the school's inaction in response to what was happening to me under their watch was due to their beliefs being inherently homophobic. And because they did think I was gay, the blame of it all lay with me. So it wasn't wrong for the other kids to point out this flaw in who I was. And if the school was to make an example of the bullies, it would feel like they were somehow justifying my perceived abhorrent nature. That's definitely what I took on board at the time.

I deserved it.

It was my fault.

There was no escape. Even when I sequestered myself into my bedroom, away from all the scrutiny and judgement, I was still left with the unchangeable reality that I was gay. My fervent prayers and deep search of my soul and conscience would never change that. As a consequence, I was suicidal for years as a teenager because I was trapped.

But inaction doesn't just make victims feel helpless. It also sends the message to the abusers that it's okay. These kids grow up without those ideas ever being challenged, and they become adults with severe and even violent feelings toward homosexuality. Their loud views get passed on to their own children, and so the cycle continues. To look at the school now, and the other schools in the Pared system that have sprouted up since my graduation, I can see that some of those very same kids who made my life a living hell are now teachers there. One of the numeraries I knew from my time at the Nairana study centre is now highly placed in the Pared school system. So despite the progress of time, their ideological bubble remains unchecked. Though more than twenty years have passed since I graduated from Redfield College, I can guarantee that there are queer children hiding within those conservative walls to this day, in their own little cages, experiencing the same harsh words, actions and vulgar opinions as I did, which chip away at their value, self-worth and will to live.

I graduated from Redfield College in 2003. Despite the ordeal, I ended up doing pretty well in my Higher School

Certificate. I had the best sleep of my life on my last day of school. I was finally free of the place and was excited to go after what *I* wanted. I had really missed the opera over the years. I missed performing. I missed acting. I had big dreams and high hopes, but I knew that no-one in my family took me seriously.

I had known what I wanted for a long time now. I had no contacts, and no clue about how I would make it happen, but I was determined to prove myself.

I wanted to be a movie star.

CHAPTER FIVE

Coming of Age

With school finally behind me, it was now time to put my money where my mouth was. My years as an opera singer had given me a passion for the performing arts and, thanks to the encouragement of my English teacher, I had developed a deep love for film and television. My parents were very much against this career, however. Though they were right in suggesting that it wasn't a stable way of making an income and had no guarantees of success, my mum's main concern was that acting was a superficial industry filled with people who only cared about their own glorification, rather than the glorification of God – which was, after all, our purpose in this earthly life.

She had always told me, almost on a daily basis, that there was no greater calling from God than to become a priest. In the months after graduating high school, her push for me to join a seminary – a college for the training of men for the priesthood – became even stronger. She spoke long and hard about each of us having a vocation in life, something that God had called for us to do, and she was certain that my vocation was the priesthood.

Any time I thought about becoming a priest, however, I would get a feeling of doom in my stomach. I was depressed by the idea and felt like it would be a waste of my life and everything I wanted to achieve with it. But I didn't trust that instinct. I didn't trust *any* of my instincts.

My instincts told me I was gay, and yet that was a mortal sin condemning me to hell. My instincts had made me want to stick up for myself against the persecution I felt at school, but that was meant to be an opportunity to 'turn the other cheek'. My instincts were for the performing arts, but that was always shot down as a superficial and 'worldly' career path – part of Satan's temptation to lure me away from the selfless and pure plan God had for me. So, yeah, I didn't trust my instincts. I always went against them because that was the only way I had been conditioned to believe I could receive love. God's love. *My family's* love.

Maybe discovering my vocation wasn't meant to be a joyous feeling but rather something that reminded me of the sacrifice of it all and, therefore, an ultimate offering of love to God?

It was a question I thought about constantly and I was at war with myself. But for the time being, I needed to go after what I wanted and prove that part of myself as legitimate. I was genuinely excited by the film industry. Thanks to my English teacher's inspiration, I had developed a fascination with directors, cinematography and film composition. I spent my free time running around with the family's handheld camera, making short films with my cousins as actors, teaching myself how to do stop-motion animation, writing music for my own short films and scouring the internet for the latest entertainment industry news.

I didn't join a seminary. But, as I didn't have a single clue how I was going to achieve my goals, and in order to keep the peace with Mum, I agreed to enrol at university in a Bachelor of Arts degree. 'You'd at least make a great teacher!' Mum sighed.

I lasted all of two months at university before I was bored out of my brain. I felt like I had wasted enough of my life languishing in institutions that weren't giving me the education I needed. It was the first time I ever rebelled, but I was too much of a coward to tell my parents that I had stopped going.

However, under the ever-vigilant eye of my grandmother, who now lived with us, I would be snitched on if I stayed at home all day. So, for months I pretended I was still going to uni.

Sometimes I'd go to the cinema and watch a couple of movies back-to-back. Sometimes I'd wander aimlessly through the local shopping centre. But more often than not, I would catch the train into the city and spend the day walking around to various film schools and acting classes to get a sense of what I needed to be doing. Eventually, I found a film school at Sydney University and signed up for night classes.

One evening, I plucked up the courage to tell my parents that I had dropped out of uni. It wasn't well received. A silence fell over the table. In typical Dad fashion, he didn't say anything but simply cleared the empty plates from the table and started to stack the dishwasher. I sat anxiously opposite my mum, who was staring daggers at me.

'You will ruin your life!' she hissed before launching into a lecture about how I was giving myself over to earthly temptations. 'There is nothing to be gained from that industry except sex, drugs and debauchery. Movie stars are all full of themselves and have no morals.'

'I don't want to do anything else,' I replied.

'I think you would make such a good priest,' she pleaded for the millionth time. 'The altar could be your ultimate stage!'

I, however, saw my career choice *as* my vocation. As someone who had experienced years of deep suicidal depression, the escapism of movies and TV had saved me on more than one occasion. I wanted to be part of that. As a stage performer, I had experienced firsthand the effects of entertainment on an audience and I wanted to continue to be of service to people in that way.

Mum, however, couldn't or *wouldn't* understand this argument. Though she too enjoyed her TV series and films, she was also unable to view the actors as anything other than their characters. When Heath Ledger played his iconic role as the Joker in *The Dark Knight*, she told me that she would be deeply ashamed if I ever played a role like that. She would hate for people to think of me as being so evil. Her ability to recognise that it was all just make-believe was simply not there. And when Heath passed away, rather than being saddened by his death, she used it as fuel for her argument.

This was evidence of the corrupting nature of Hollywood, and she said her fear was that I too would one day be found dead on a mattress in an empty apartment.

In her mind, the only actor who wasn't bad news was Jim Caviezel because he had played Jesus in *The Passion of the Christ*.

After a lengthy argument in which my dad said nothing, Mum eventually slumped back in her seat wearing a look of extreme disappointment. 'If this is what you really want, you're doing it on your own,' she said. 'I can't help you!'

So that was what I did.

I started working at a petrol station and soon got a second job at a cinema. The petrol station was mind-numbingly boring, but I loved working at the movies. The smell of my bedroom, after a long double shift, was a cocktail of gasoline and popcorn. But the work meant I could start putting money aside to seek out the training I wanted. Shortly after this, I successfully auditioned for a two-year part-time screen acting course at the National Institute of Dramatic Art (NIDA). I wanted to purge myself of the melodramatic acting habits I had developed over my opera career and learn the subtleties and techniques of acting on camera. But I hadn't come out of my shell yet. I was painfully shy and really only used to the sheltered world I had grown up in, so this course was a real challenge for me. Breaking down the barriers of my inhibitions took a lot, and I was confronted with characters and scenes that I simply didn't understand because I had no worldly experience.

I was also too self-conscious and awkward to stay after class and socialise. After my time at Redfield, I distrusted people and class groups. When the rest of the acting class headed to the pub for drinks, I would sit in my car around the corner and eat a Picnic bar and a bag of chips, and drink a can of Coke before driving to the church to play the organ for Saturday evening mass, a duty I had been performing for several years already.

As the weeks went on, I started to find pieces of my personality and even started to build connections with my classmates, with whom I had initially been very standoffish. I was meeting a different kind of person in this environment, and there didn't seem to be a judgemental bone in their bodies. I started to realise that sometimes I made people laugh, that some people didn't care that I wasn't the most butch guy on the planet and that maybe there was something likeable about me after all.

This class was one of the most foundational experiences in my life. It started everything for me, not least of which was the beginning of my self-confidence. One day during class, instead of eating my lunch in a corner by myself, I decided to join the rest of the group. One of my classmates, a guy by the name of Chris Hemsworth, started to chat with me about what my hopes and dreams were as an actor.

'So, where do you see yourself going with this?' he asked.

I don't need to describe how intensely attractive he was. I couldn't bring myself to make eye contact with him while I answered. 'Well, I guess the ultimate goal is to be in my own movie that I've written, directed and written the score for,' I replied. 'You know, Clint Eastwood.'

'Wow, that's impressive,' he said, chuckling at the loftiness of my ambition. 'How do you plan on making that happen?'

'Well,' I replied nervously, 'I kinda thought I might start out like you. Do a bit of time on *Home and Away* and then maybe give Hollywood a crack?'

This amused Chris, as it was literally his own plan mirrored back to him. *Home and Away* had been going through a phase of casting super-jacked guys lately, something that I was secretly very appreciative of. I was quite a bit heavier at the time, having never set foot in a gym, and Chris suggested that I should think about working out a bit.

'Look, I'm not the best actor in the world, mate,' he said, patting me on the back and making my every hair stand on end from the thrill of his physical contact. 'That's why I'm doing this course. But I'm pretty sure the reason I got the gig on *Homers* is because my character's a shirtless surfer guy.'

There was nothing conceited about the way he said this to me. I saw his point, and the next day I joined a gym. Within a year, I'd lost about 15 kilograms.

By then I had built up a lot more confidence. I was learning so much in my acting classes and had grown significantly. I wasn't as shy, I had a social life, I was feeling positive about my appearance and had started to buy my own clothes, much to my mother's chagrin. She had watched my transformation unfold and she wasn't happy about it. Any time I went to the gym, she would tell me I was being vain. She would point out larger or unconventional-looking actors and say, 'See, he's an actor.' She would bring up Anthony Hopkins and Dustin Hoffman as examples of accomplished actors who didn't need to be *hot* to be successful. But it wasn't like I'd be starting out with their kinds of roles. And though physical appearance absolutely does not equal talent, there is no denying that appearance plays a part in casting, especially twenty years ago. I just wanted to have as much going for me as possible.

I spent the next few years working hard and putting my money toward any acting courses and workshops I could find. I allowed my tunnel vision on my career aspirations to distract me from the 'gay' thing and continued to hide my sexuality. I was adamant to myself that I would never give in to the temptation; however, I did imagine a life where I was able to kiss a fella and, dare I dream it, be happy for the rest of my life with a male partner. If I was ever caught out accidentally looking at a cute guy in the gym mirror, I would be flooded with fear that it was the devil tempting me. Apart from a regular need to delete the internet search history on the family computer, my deep, dark secret was something I was prepared to take with me to the grave.

I continued to play the organ at various parishes for Sunday mass, and I even started to lead a children's choir at my local Franciscan parish with a former classmate who was there training for the priesthood. I hoped that these acts meant that I could somehow atone to God for my sinful homosexual attractions, and that he would bestow enough grace onto me so I could continue to ward off temptations. This outwardly devout appearance also helped keep the secret under wraps to my family.

However, my efforts to prove myself were thwarted one day when Mum found gay pornography in my bedroom. She had been snooping in my room and had been very thorough in her endeavour, because the small stash that I had – a magazine and a DVD – was buried deep within my bottom desk drawer. I was twenty-one years old and had just arrived home from a long shift at the movie theatre. As soon as I opened the front door, I heard her call me from the dining room.

'Tim, is that you? Come here now!' Her voice shook.

I assumed from how emotional she sounded that something must have happened to my grandmother. However, upon entering the room, I saw that she had ripped out each page of the magazine and laid them over the dining room table. My heart dropped to my ankles and my head filled with white noise. Dad stood at the kitchen bench, avoiding eye contact. Mum stood beside the table, quivering with rage.

'Is this who you are?' she shouted at me. 'Is this what you've become?'

I was blindsided. I couldn't think of anything to say.

She held the DVD next to her face, featuring three exceptionally muscular men at full excitement, if you catch my drift. 'Is this what you like?' she yelled.

'No?' was all I could manage.

'I never thought my son could be this perverted. I'm so ashamed of you!'

I continued to just stand there in silence.

'I knew this would happen if I let you be corrupted by the world. Have I failed you as a mother?'

'I'm sorry,' I replied meekly.

'This is wrong, Tim. It's *wrong*! And it stops now!'

I nodded.

'Where did you even get it?' She shook her head. 'No, I don't want to know.' She threw me a garbage bag. 'It's going in there, and you're taking it to the garbage bin outside. I don't want something so demonic in my house. This is a house of God.'

It felt like an eternity as I picked each of the magazine pages up from the table. I was struggling to see through the tears in my eyes. My ears were ringing, my heart was thumping, and every nerve ending in my body felt like it was on fire.

When I returned from disposing of the contraband, I sat down with Mum in the living room. I told her that I wasn't gay. Lie. I told her that it was a mere curiosity. Also a lie. I told her that after years of being accused of being gay at school, and never having any interest from girls, I had merely bought the pornography to see if I really *was* gay.

'And?' she asked.

'No, Mum, I'm not. I didn't like it.' More lies. I had liked it very much.

'Good,' she said. 'Because if you were, we'd have to do something about it.'

That was the one and only time we ever spoke about it, but afterward I would always catch her looking at me with a desperate worry in her eyes.

The thing was, I still didn't want to be gay. I was still praying very deeply each day that God would 'fix' me. I had no intention of ever acting on my homosexuality. I was focused on my career and would try to bargain with God that I would be quite happy to be single and celibate for the rest of my life if I could just achieve the career that I had my heart set on. But, clearly, I needed to redouble my efforts in front of my family in order to keep the wool over their eyes. I started to date a girl I worked with at the cinema, hoping that this would settle any lingering fears. She was a lovely person and we got along well. She was tall and very pretty, and some of the 'lads' would congratulate me for 'pulling a chick like her'. After a few months, however, I started to feel intensely guilty about it. Though we had been together for several months, we had never once kissed. I simply wasn't interested in kissing her, and I knew that I was merely using this poor girl for my own selfish needs. It really was quite a misogynistic thing to do, and it didn't sit well with me. Shortly after my twenty-second birthday, I broke things off with her, using my focus on my career as an excuse. I hated that I hurt her feelings so much, but it was the right thing to do.

By this time, I had spent every cent I had earned on my acting pursuits, but no agencies in Australia showed any interest in me. The Australian film and television industry is small, with nowhere near the budgets of Hollywood. Therefore, it makes sense that the same people would continue to be cast, leaving very little room for newcomers. And any fresh talent that was successful in getting agency representation was often left for months or years without any work to justify their training or ability. For someone like me, it was almost impossible to get any attention from anyone. Especially because the headshots I had spent almost $600 on were, in truth, utterly horrendous. But one day I found out that a huge HBO series called *The Pacific*, produced by Steven Spielberg and Tom Hanks, was to be filmed in Melbourne, and they needed a plethora of young male actors to be part of the show. I wanted a shot, but without an agent to get me an audition, I had to find other ways to be seen.

After a lot of internet sleuthing, I found out who the casting director was and I sent them my headshot and showreel every single day. For weeks. I then called them each day to see if they had received my delivery. After about a month of this, the casting director called me and asked me to come in and show them what I was made of. I had a short meeting with them, where I felt very scrutinised, but was offered an audition for the project to see if my belligerent tenacity was matched by any actual talent.

I learned my lines back to front. I practised the delivery of each individual word a million times. I learned the lines of the other characters, and stood in my bedroom filming myself performing the scenes over and over, and would then watch each take back and critique my performance. If I didn't like the way my head tilted when I said a particular line, I would change it. If a certain sigh or hand gesture felt unnecessary, I would work to perfect it. I analysed every minute detail of how I performed the audition scenes so that when I walked into the room, I could be confident that I was going to prove myself. I spent almost an extra thousand dollars on an acting coach to assist me with my preparation and slept very little in the days leading up to my audition. This was the biggest opportunity I had ever had, and was exactly what I had been dreaming of for years. I was *not* going to blow it.

While I don't recommend this kind of preparation or pressure for any audition, it ultimately resulted in multiple callbacks over the next few months. In fact, I came tantalisingly close to one of the lead roles. After several weeks of continual auditions for the project, I ended up doing a screen test for the HBO producers. I walked into a room filled with powerful Hollywood execs. The pressure was extreme, but I knew I couldn't fault my dedication to the work. Ultimately, however, I was unsuccessful. Rather than feeling disappointment, I was proud of myself for getting so far. Not bad for a sheltered introvert with outrageous goals to have made it all the way to a meeting with HBO executives and producers. After so many years of setbacks and doubt from my own family, my pipe dream suddenly seemed tangible. I was filled with confidence that I wasn't wasting my time in pursuing this career and I was able to leverage the success of that audition process to finally gain an agent, thanks to the kind words offered by the casting director who had noticed my drive and the work I had put in.

A few months later, the same casting director requested me to audition for a mystery film called 'Project X'. The character I was going for was called 'SS'. I was at work at the movie theatre when the audition request came through and, by the time I got off work, I had less than twelve hours to prepare for it. Though everything about this audition was being kept under wraps, I had an inkling of what the project was. What I had been sent for the audition was an action scene in which 'SS' loses his red-tinted glasses during a tussle and laser beams shoot out of his eyes. I knew that the latest instalment of the *X-Men* franchise was being shot in Sydney (because I spent literally every waking moment of my life keeping up to date with current goings-on in the film industry) and that Cyclops, whose real name is Scott Summers ('SS'), was a superhero in the *X-Men* universe. Just like I had done with my previous audition for this casting director, and under the weight of what I was auditioning for, I stayed up all night rehearsing the scene a million different ways. I filmed myself acting 'shocked' and 'scared' over and over again, and I spent hours trying to style my hair the same way as James Marsden, who had played the role in the previous three films. I wanted to look the part and be prepared for anything.

The next morning, I arrived at the casting director's office with a face full of make-up to hide the dark circles from my sleepless night. I tried to ignore the dozen or so other guys in the waiting room, most of whom I recognised from various movies, TV shows and modelling campaigns, and all of whom were exceptionally gorgeous. Auditions are hard, not just because of the level of preparation and the restrictions of the audition environment, but also because of all the hope that is attached. Each audition represents a life-changing possibility, but attaching too much hope to it can be emotionally damaging. Not only that, but you have to try and block out the intimidation you feel when you see the sea of other actors entering the audition room before you. After the audition, I attempted to immediately put it out of my mind. I will say, however, that unlike most of my auditions, I walked out with no regrets and felt confident that I had a legitimate shot at this one.

A few days later, I was called to Fox Studios in Sydney, as it was known at the time, to do a 'stunt audition', which was something I had absolutely no idea how to prepare for. As I walked through the studio backlot, I saw Hugh Jackman entering his trailer and couldn't quite believe that I was getting so close to something so big. I spent the next few hours working with the stunt team, workshopping an action sequence in the film. They showed me how to run on camera. They taught me how to do a flip mid-air. And they filmed everything. Eventually I was introduced to the director, Gavin Hood, who had won an Academy Award for Best Foreign Language Film in 2006 for his film *Tsotsi*. We had a brief meeting in which he viewed the videos of me performing the stunts. We talked briefly about the character and his direction. It was a Friday, and he told me that a decision would be made over the weekend and I would hear back on Monday.

It was the longest weekend of my life. I was indulging in the fantasy of my dreams coming true while also expecting to be monumentally crushed by rejection. I begged my friends to spend time with me as a distraction from my own brain, though I didn't tell them why. At night, I sneaked into my grandmother's bedroom while she slept and hid my phone in her drawer so that I wouldn't be tempted to scroll through any pornography and masturbate. I didn't want to displease God at this pivotal time and was praying to him every moment. God knew the desires in my heart. God knew my dreams, and how much I wanted this opportunity. Though I knew I had worked hard to reach that point and had nailed my auditions, it wasn't up to me. Talent and drive meant nothing without dutiful faith. This decision wasn't in my hands, or even in the hands of the studio or the director. It was up to God. Therefore, I had to avoid temptation and offer up my sacrifice to him in order to receive his favour.

Monday came and went without any news. I tried to make peace with the letdown. After a restless night, I took myself to the gym early on Tuesday morning to clear my head. I was in the gym locker room after a long swim when I finally decided to check my phone for an update. My agents had left a voicemail casually informing me that I was required at the studio as soon as possible for a wardrobe fitting, because I had booked the role and my first night on set was in just one week!

I walked out of the gym in a haze. When I sat in my car, I relistened to the voicemail over and over, just to be sure I hadn't misheard. I had spent so many years wanting exactly this, and had felt held back from my dreams for such a long time. Despite the obstacles, I had clung onto a blind belief in myself that even I didn't know the source of. But in that moment, sitting in my car on a cold Tuesday morning outside the Castle Hill RSL gym, I realised that I had never *truly* believed that it would ever happen. Now that it had, I was in too much shock to comprehend it. The message had said that I wasn't allowed to tell anyone, but I called my best mate Dave and told him. We had met during the screen acting course at NIDA and had stayed really close since. Though another actor with the same goals as myself, it is a testament to the kind of guy he is that he was nothing but overjoyed for me. In fact, it was his exuberant reaction that snapped me out of my trance. Realisation flooded my senses and I laugh-cried for about ten minutes before realising I had a job to do and was expected at the studio asap.

Coldplay's song 'Viva la Vida' was the latest hit single at the time and I listened to it on loop as I drove to the studio. It was the happiest morning of my life, and I got several looks from passing drivers while I belted the song at full voice, bouncing up and down in the driver's seat. For once in my life, I didn't care what anyone else thought of me.

This wasn't just any role in any film. I was playing a superhero in a Hollywood blockbuster action franchise. Realistically, a role like this would only be possible after years of paying my dues in smaller productions. Though I wanted this, I had never expected it to happen like this. The first *X-Men* film had been released when I was fifteen years old. As an unpopular kid, I hadn't had friends to see it with at the movies, but it had been the hot topic among my classmates. When I convinced my parents to rent the movie when the DVD was released, it was my first introduction to a superhero world outside of the 1960s *Batman* series and the *Superman* films of the 1970s and 80s.

As a teenage boy, I had been the target market for the film, and I had loved it. The action was cool, their powers ignited my imagination and I was very taken by James Marsden, who played Scott Summers, aka Cyclops. He was so handsome and dapper. Closeted young Tim thought he was the most beautiful man he had ever seen, and wished to one day grow up and be him. And then that day, as I sat screaming Coldplay at the top of my lungs behind my steering wheel, I realised that I *had* grown up, and I *was* him.

CHAPTER SIX

The Career Curse

I signed a non-disclosure agreement when I was officially offered the role in *X-Men* and therefore couldn't tell anyone what I was doing. I had to tell my job that I needed a significant period of time off and wouldn't be able to tell them the reason why. And apart from my parents and best friend, no-one else knew why I was all of a sudden so mysteriously busy and unusually euphoric.

A week later, after a whirlwind of costume fittings, rehearsals, plaster casts being made of my head and trying on over 400 pairs of sunglasses, I sat in the back of a boat carving its way through Sydney Harbour at dusk toward Cockatoo Island, where I would be filming for the next few nights. The producers and director were waiting for me when I disembarked. I found myself shaking hands with Hugh Jackman and hearing him greet me by name after spending the last four years selling tickets to his movies. I was shown to a trailer with my name on the door. Then, at about 1 am, with a camera in my face in front of a crew of hundreds, the director called 'Action!' and I was doing the thing I had dreamed of for almost thirteen years. It was thrilling.

Over the next few weeks, I lived in the fantasy world that I had never thought would become a reality. I was involved in some major scenes in the film, including some big action sequences in the studio. I couldn't help but wonder how the kids who had mercilessly bashed me in my teen years for being an effeminate faggot would react when they realised that I was now a superhero. It sounds stupid to put it that way, but they say success is the best revenge, and this felt like a major 'fuck you' to everyone who had ever doubted me. I shared scenes with not only Hugh but also Ryan Reynolds, Liev Schreiber and even Sir Patrick Stewart. Every day on set was a surreal fantasy come to life, and I cherished every second of it. My jubilance, however, was cut short almost as soon as it had begun.

The week after I wrapped filming and had resumed working my day job at the movie theatre, Mum asked to speak with me privately. We went into my piano room and sat in silence for a few minutes, she in one of the comfy armchairs and me perched on my piano stool. She looked pale, and fidgeted with one of the cushions before looking up at me and saying, 'There's something I need to tell you.'

'Okay ...' I replied nervously.

'I have to go into hospital for an operation,' she said.

'Oh.' I could feel my heart starting to race.

'I have to get a hysterectomy,' she continued. 'The doctors found a tumor. I have stage four ovarian cancer.'

Time stopped in that moment. No words came to my mind. We sat there for a few minutes staring at each other. She had always been such a strong, self-assured woman, but I had never seen her look so scared.

I wish I had responded better. But nothing will ever prepare you for news like that. I literally said nothing. Eventually, she stood up, held my hand for a moment and then walked out of the room. I didn't move for a while. It took some time to absorb what she had said, and even then I was too overwhelmed to know how to process it. I sat there for about half an hour before swivelling around on my piano stool and pouring my feelings into the keys. I wish I had given her a hug. I wish I had shown more emotion. I wish I had told her I loved her and that I would always be there for her. But the moment had passed, and the only thing I could do was vow to myself that I would take care of her.

When I went downstairs for breakfast the morning of her operation, Mum looked the most frail that I had ever seen her. I asked her what the plan was, and she told me that Dad was going to drop her off at the hospital and she would just figure it out from there. I insisted that Dad accompany her. He, however, said he was far too busy with work to do that. That didn't make sense to me. How could he be so callous? How could he not see how terrified his wife was? And how could he not want to be by her side every step of the way? I said I would call in sick from work and go with her. She wouldn't hear of it, but I didn't let it go. I was furious with Dad for being so blasé about something so monumental.

I pushed and I pushed, and eventually, reluctantly, Dad agreed that he would go to work later in the day once Mum was settled in the hospital.

I went to work as scheduled, but within an hour of my shift, the gravity of the situation hit me. Perhaps I had been in denial until that point. Perhaps I had been ignoring my feelings. Perhaps it was the thought of her on an operating table at that moment. But sitting behind the box office counter, selling tickets to movies … I had a very public meltdown. A customer had been yelling at me about the movie ticket price, and I exploded in front of everyone. I called the customer a cunt – to her face (which was extremely out of character) – and burst into hysterical tears. I couldn't control my emotions and was immediately removed from public view. My co-workers had no idea what was going on. I hadn't told them about Mum. All they knew was that I had vanished for a few months, had returned and was now wailing in a corner after a simple customer complaint. A co-worker put her arms around me, which only made it worse. I hid in the back storeroom for hours, doing stocktake for the cinema, trying to numb myself to the situation. When I got home that afternoon, I wrote a piece of music on the piano as music had always been my best form of self-expression. It's called 'Stillness'. I still play it to this day. It reminds me of the hauntingly numb sorrow that I felt at the time, that words just can't do justice to.

Mum's tumour had ruptured her ovary and was one of the largest the oncologist had ever seen. It had also spread to her pelvis and, though the medical team tried to remove all of the cancer, it just wasn't possible. After she recovered from the operation, she started a very aggressive chemotherapy regimen, which took a massive toll on her body. Apart from the expected loss of hair, she dropped so much weight so fast. It was devastating to see, but I knew I had to be strong for her. Dad was working long hours, including several trips interstate for weeks at a time, so I kept her company as much as I could and did whatever she needed. I felt so sorry for her. She was such a strong woman, and now her strength was being robbed from her.

A few months later, I was flown to Canada to complete filming on *X-Men* and spent the month of January 2009 in Vancouver. I was supposedly living the Hollywood dream, being flown around the world and staying in fancy hotels while shooting the latest action blockbuster with some of the biggest stars in the world. But I was still that quiet, awkward, shy and closeted kid who found the world scary and intimidating. I was also preoccupied with worry about Mum. When I wasn't filming on set, I spent most of that trip alone in my hotel room, and talked on the phone with her for hours every day.

I returned to work at the cinema after I got back from Vancouver. A few weeks later, the poster for *X-Men Origins: Wolverine* was released. I was on shift one night when a delivery arrived of new posters for us to display. As I removed a poster from its cylinder and started to unroll it, I saw Hugh Jackman's face with a giant 'X' behind him.

And as I continued to unroll it, to my utter shock, I saw my *own* face. I had never posed for a poster photo and had absolutely no idea I would be featured. I had been half-expecting my scenes to end up on the cutting room floor. Instead, there I was, on the poster for that secret thing I wasn't allowed to tell anyone about. I put it on display, gathered my co-workers and stood beside myself long enough for them to realise. It was a proud moment and I finally had some bragging rights.

A few weeks later, Mum went into remission. My movie poster was everywhere and a film trailer that heavily featured me had been released. With fewer worries at home and a huge opportunity before me, I turned my sights to Tinseltown.

This brings us to where we began: the Los Angeles premiere of the film in April of 2009. I worked at the movie theatre right up until my departure – I really didn't want to sell tickets to my own movie and I was determined not to miss attending my very own Hollywood premiere. The trip cost me thousands, but it felt like a calculated move.

X-Men Origins: Wolverine went number one worldwide and raked in box office gold. With the success of the film, and having played a popular character in it, I felt it was worth spending more time trying to leverage more career opportunities from the exposure. I therefore spent several very lonely months in LA. I didn't know a soul in Hollywood. My Australian agents had set up meetings with other agencies and management companies over there, and I was getting auditions, but I knew absolutely no-one. Outside of the meetings and auditions, I spent my time by myself. I would go to the gym, watch a movie, and then head back to my apartment above a flower shop in Burbank and wait for another audition to come through. After a few weeks of this, Mum's cancer returned. She had to start another round of chemo and I just wanted to go home and be by her side.

A few days after learning about Mum's relapse, I received a request to tape an audition for a new Australian television series called *Dance Academy*. It was being shot in my hometown of Sydney. As is standard, I had very little time to prepare, so without knowing much about the project, I learned my lines, taped the audition and sent it off. The next day, my agents were urging me to return to Australia. The producers wanted to meet me in person, which, given their level of interest and how close it was to the start of production, was almost a guarantee of a job offer. I was delighted to return home. I had wanted to do the right thing by my career by staying in LA, but this *Dance Academy* show was giving me the chance to take care of both my career *and* my mother.

Jet-lagged and with absolutely no idea what I was really walking into, I turned up to a dance studio in Artarmon a couple of days later. I met with the producers and director and filmed several scenes with some actors who had already been cast. A few hours later, I was told that my audition had been successful. I knew very little about the show. My agents had told me it was 'a kids show with dancing', so I was expecting it to be something like *The Wiggles* or *Hi-5*. Though I knew the two audition scenes that I had prepared,

I hadn't been sent any scripts so I was flying blind. I didn't really care, though. I was happy to have an excuse to be back home, and at least it was a television job that kept my career hopes alive.

But *Dance Academy* ended up being so much more than that. It was a fully scripted drama that beautifully depicted the awkward insecurities of teenage life through the lens of a ballet academy. I was twenty-three when I was cast as a seventeen-year-old in the show, but it felt like I was finally getting the chance to attend the performing arts school I had wished for when I was my character's age. The show provided the perfect playground for me to relearn a few things, and I felt comfortable playing a character so much younger than I was because of how developmentally stunted I felt due to my own upbringing and education. Additionally, I still had so much to learn about acting on camera, and I needed to meet more people from the industry who could boost my confidence and allow me to continue my professional and personal development. I made some of my best friends in the world over the following six months of the shoot. My co-stars were a buoyant bunch of exceptionally talented teens. They were smart and funny, kind and nurturing. I was in awe of how confident and self-assured they were, jealous of how invested their families were in their careers and, though I was several years their elder, they all seemed so much more mature than me. I feel like we all grew up together on that show, and bonding with them was such a beautiful distraction from the constant worry about Mum. It wasn't just the cast, however. The producers, directors, writers and crew were all part of the family unit, and it became a safe space for me to come further out of my shell.

I learned a lot thanks to *Dance Academy.* Not least of which is that I absolutely cannot dance. I hate to disappoint any fans out there, but I am beyond incapable of dancing. During the first week of the shoot, I had a choreography rehearsal for a hip-hop routine I was meant to do. When I returned to the studio, I bumped into my co-stars Dena Kaplan and Alicia Banit. They asked me to show them what I had just learned. Look, they *tried* not to be disrespectful, but I could see that they were battling tears of laughter behind their encouraging smiles. The next day, after footage from my rehearsal had been reviewed by the producers, a revision of that script came out, and my character was no longer required to dance in it.

It didn't help matters when, during a scene in which it was unavoidable for my character to dance, I somehow managed to pass wind with great heft while attempting something called a barrel roll, sending the studio into chaotic screams of laughter as I crawled into the corner of the set and hid behind a curtain.

The rest of the cast were incredible dancers who had trained for years at performing arts and dance schools. They constantly blew me away with their talent, but after a time, I felt like there was more that I could contribute to the show other than being the main character's object of desire. Eventually, I pitched to the writers that I could play piano and asked if we could incorporate that into the show. They didn't seem convinced at first, so I sent them a piece I had written when I was seventeen years old, called 'Hero', and said that we could use it in the show. Soon, they wrote it into an episode. Finally, I got to show off a little, and in so doing I was able to share one of my original musical compositions with the world. For so many years, my passions had been the source of my torment, but now I was surrounded by people who appreciated my abilities and had been provided with a platform to broadcast them on an international scale. I had been able to single-handedly prove my worth.

My confidence grew during filming. I had finally found something that made me feel completely whole for the first time since my days with the Australian Opera Company almost a decade earlier.

My memories from *Dance Academy*, along with the lifelong friendships I made, will always give me the warm fuzzies whenever I think about them. At the time, however, I was still desperately hiding my sexuality. I was paranoid playing this 'golden boy' love interest. I had been the unpopular loner eating my lunch in the toilets in high school; could I ever be believable as the popular heart-throb? I was incredibly self-conscious about how I delivered every line, how I stood, how my posture looked, how *masculine* I was coming across. So I dissected everything with extreme precision, never truly feeling present in the moment, because what if something about me came across as 'gay' while the cameras were rolling? I was going to be on TV screens across the world, no longer hiding in toilet cubicles, so I needed to sell my heterosexuality. In my opinion, however, my determination to come across as 'unquestionably straight' made my performance quite stiff. This kind of worked for my character, who was a bit aloof and arrogant, but I always questioned whether I was really fooling anyone.

Dance Academy was such an unexpected gift. It was such a different show to what I had originally perceived it to be, and though we finished filming with a quiet confidence that we had made something really special, there were no guarantees that anyone else would get it. Despite that, however, I was very excited for it to be released and spent the few months after filming anxiously waiting for it to be shared with the world. Once again, however, as I was coming down from a huge career high, something happened that brought me crashing back down to earth.

In the weeks leading up to the show's premiere, the producers asked the cast to send them photos or video footage of us performing as kids, as they were putting together a 'making of' feature and wanted to show our careers since we were little. I knew my dad had several folders of family photos on the home computer, and I figured that there would be some pictures from my opera days somewhere in there. I started searching through his folders hoping to find something to contribute. What I found, however, was something entirely different. While digging through his myriad files, I accidentally stumbled on his mobile phone back-up. Without realising what I had opened, I soon discovered that I was reading his text messages and that he was, in fact, having an affair. And the object of his affections was my mum's cousin ... who also happened to be my godmother.

Unwilling to believe what I was seeing, I frantically searched through everything. I read all the text messages, opened every photo, read every email, hoping that I would be proven wrong, but all this did was confirm it. The hypocrisy of it all made my blood boil. I had berated myself my whole life for my devious and sinful nature. I had prayed for forgiveness and vowed to repress it until my dying day. I lived a life of resisting temptation, filled with hidden shame for something that I had been born with and could never change about myself. And yet, not one but *two* people from my holier-than-thou Catholic family were actively participating in something that was not only sinful *by choice*, but also, unlike homosexuality, deeply hurtful to others. My 'perfect Catholic family' suddenly felt like a soap opera: the closeted gay kid in a dance show, with a cousin/godmother who was secretly having an affair with the father while the mother was dying of cancer upstairs.

Suddenly, my dad's seeming ambivalence the day of Mum's operation made sense, along with the fact that he appeared so absent all the time. He *had* been spending a lot of time at my godmother's place, helping with housework, fixing her computer and even taking her garbage bins to the kerb. I had never been so angry in all my life, and yet I didn't want Mum to know. Her body was already breaking due to her illness; I didn't want to break her heart as well.

So I kept my father's secret. I never told him, or my godmother, that I knew. The only person in the family I told was my sister. She had gotten married when she was twenty, and she lived in the Blue Mountains with her husband and kids. I drove immediately to her place because I simply couldn't handle this on my own, and she agreed with me that, unless Mum managed a full recovery, we would never tell them what we knew. And I, for my part, made sure that I would step up to the plate and be the man in Mum's life she *could* rely on.

I took Mum to her chemotherapy appointments and sat with her for the long hours it took to pump her full of poison. I would lie awake at night, hearing her vomit for hours on end, each retch like a dagger to the heart. I would drive her to and from mass every day, make her meals and prepare afternoon tea for her plethora of well-meaning visitors. My grandmother, who still lived with us, had recently had a stroke and needed round-the-clock care. Though several cousins also lived with us and shared the load, I took on my mum's role as one of Granny's carers so that Mum only had to worry about herself. However, being the woman she was, she always pushed through the pain and weakness she was experiencing and continued to be at my grandmother's every beck and call.

On weekends, my godmother would come over for Sunday lunch and I hated sitting at the dining table knowing the truth behind the lies. She would often gift Mum items of her old clothing. It was perverse to me that Mum would be walking around in front of Dad with clothes that had belonged to his mistress. On one of these occasions, there was a piece of lingerie in among the clothes my godmother had so graciously given Mum. Mum thought it was hysterical that this celibate single woman who lived with her mother had lingerie. How little she knew. But I felt a subtle satisfaction in making fun of my godmother in front of Dad, knowing that he wouldn't be able to come to her defence.

Mum went in and out of remission several times. She was put on all the trial drugs and experimental procedures possible. Meanwhile, I continued to act. *Dance Academy* had become a huge hit, and I had been cast in smaller roles on other television shows as well, including a stint on Chris Hemsworth's very own *Home and Away* before starting up a second season of *Dance Academy*. But by midway through 2011, Mum had reached the end of the line.

We were sitting in front of the TV in the living room, just the two of us, when she suddenly turned off the TV and, with the same sense of foreboding as before, said she needed to tell me something.

There was nothing more that could be done.

She was going to die.

Again, I wish I had done more. I wish I had learned my lesson from the first time. But I can't describe the feeling that came over me. It was like my entire brain became nothing but white noise. I do remember that I was trying to remain strong, and yet I couldn't stop myself from crying. The worst part about it was that she felt responsible. She felt guilty that she was dying, and that she had to tell me. I could see that on her face but, try as I did to hold back the tears, they fell of their own accord. I didn't want her to see because it would only make her feel worse, so I simply walked out of the room and left her there.

My time on *Dance Academy* was also coming to an end. My character was leaving Australia to pursue his dancing career overseas. The day I filmed my character's final scene was about two weeks after I found out about mum's prognosis. I was about to say goodbye to her, and I was also about to say goodbye to this beautiful show and all the wonderful people who had been a second family to me.

Before filming my final scene, I sat on the edge of the wharf in front of the Sydney Harbour Bridge. It was early morning, and the rising sun cast amber ripples across the water. I listened to a sad song while the crew set up for the scene, and when it was ready to be shot, I approached the director and said, 'Let's not do a rehearsal. Let's just shoot it. Do my close-up, I'm ready.' The scene itself hadn't called for tears, and I hadn't planned that it would – I just knew that I was in the perfect headspace to film. My character was saying goodbye to his best friends and leaving behind things that he had cherished. I knew that all I had to do was stand there and say the words. How I was feeling would do the rest. The director called action, and that scene was the first time as an actor that I felt I gave a real, genuine performance.

I still remained the best of friends with the cast, and I came back to the show a couple of times for cameo appearances, but apart from that, I opted out of working for the next few months so that I could spend every second with Mum. It was the most difficult time in my life. I was stressed beyond measure, I wasn't sleeping, and I harboured a deep resentment toward my dad.

One day during this period, I had spent a few hours with some friends and, when I got home, discovered that Mum had been snooping in my room again. I'm not sure what she was hoping to find – more porn, perhaps? But I had become way too good at covering my tracks by then. I will admit, however, that I was quite a messy person, and my room was an absolute pigsty. She was furious with me for being so untidy and shouted, 'How many times do I ask you to clean your room? Clearly you don't love me!'

With the amount of care I was giving her, the secret I was covering up for Dad, the sleepless nights and my utter heartbreak that she was dying before my eyes, her words were some of the most offensive I had ever heard. In a heat of red mist, and with misplaced aggression, I shouted back, 'You're a fucking bitch!'

We never swore in our house. As you know, even 'shut up' was a curse that required a mouthful of soap. I instantly regretted my words, but before I could apologise, my father, who had overheard the argument from the kitchen, came running out and yelled, 'How dare you speak to your mother like that!'

All of the anger, all of the resentment, all of the hypocrisy washed over me. How dare *he* pretend like he cared about her?

I could have said it. I could have blown the lid off the entire secret. The words were at the tip of my tongue and I could have blurted them out at any second. But I didn't. I bit my tongue, ran to my room and slammed the door so hard that a piece of the frame came loose from the wall.

The next morning, Mum tapped on my door.

'I don't think you're coping very well with my illness,' she said. 'I think it would be a good idea for you to see a therapist.'

Though she had no clue about the extent of what I was dealing with, I agreed. I did need to speak to someone about everything that I was keeping to myself and was truly grateful for the opportunity. She knew a psychologist who she had recommended to others in the past, and she had already taken the liberty of booking me an appointment. I wasn't surprised by this. Whenever Mum had a suggestion, you could always be sure that her mind was already made up. And the appointment she had set was happening that very morning.

We apologised to each other for the fight from the day before, and I made sure she knew that I loved her. We got into my car and headed out for my appointment. But upon arriving at his office, I discovered that this therapist wasn't exactly a shining example of professionals in his field. And definitely not someone I could open up to ...

CHAPTER SEVEN

The Therapist

It was one of the messiest offices I had ever seen. The desk more closely resembled a big city skyline, with piles of printouts towering precariously across every inch of mahogany real estate. More papers were stacked above his filing cabinets, across his bookshelves, on top of chairs and even strewn across the floor. In among all that chaos, religious pictures and statues held pride of place. Sitting in a large, velvety armchair, the psychologist smiled at me and told me with a sense of pride that he knew I was a Redfield boy.

He immediately identified himself as a follower of Opus Dei. His smile, and the revelation that I was apparently with *one of my own*, was no doubt meant to comfort me. But I immediately became distrustful. It had been almost eight years since I graduated from Redfield. Though our family was still very much entrenched in that world, I thought that I had personally left their constant surveillance behind me in a trail of dust. I had assumed that I would be meeting with an unbiased third party, someone who I could share everything with. But knowing full well the beliefs that he would have, I also knew that my deep, dark, faggy secret was not something I could freely talk about.

The room with all its clutter now felt smaller and darker. The dust in the air seemed to hang in stasis, and I instantly became suspicious of the true motives behind why I was there. This therapy session had started to feel more like an ambush.

Mum had spoken with him privately for half an hour before I was ushered in. I had sat in the waiting room, filling out a mental health questionnaire, with a picture of the Sacred Heart of Jesus staring down at me from the wall. Though I had never officially come out to my mum, I knew that she *knew*. She had never once brought it up since 'porngate' and, though she had accepted my denial from years earlier, and had met my ex-girlfriend, I knew that I had never really fooled her. Since that mortifying incident with the pornography, she had watched me like a hawk. She was constantly going through my belongings and would open my mail, including any packages that were addressed to me. As my acting career started to take off, exposing me to a wider variety of people with 'alternative lifestyle choices', she became increasingly concerned about some of the friendships and working relationships I was developing. She was constantly on the lookout for anyone that she felt could corrupt me.

One of the head writers on *Dance Academy* was a married gay man. He had invited the cast and producers to his home one weekend for a luncheon get-together.

'Whose place is it you're going to?' Mum had asked.

'Greg's,' I said.

'Greg? But isn't he the gross one?' she said with a look of concern.

I bristled. 'What do you mean "gross"? Greg's lovely!'

'Didn't you say he's married to a man?' she replied.

'Yep,' I responded curtly.

'I don't think you should go to that,' she said matter-of-factly.

'Mum, it's a work thing. I'm going.'

So I knew that her suspicions of me had been eating away at her over the years, and I was wary of what she had been saying to the psychologist before I stepped into his office. So, as I sat opposite him, it felt like the walls were closing in on me.

'Let's start with a prayer,' he said, and prayed a quick 'Our Father', 'Hail Mary' and 'Glory Be'. He only took a passing glance at my mental health questionnaire, in which I had indicated my high levels of stress, depression, anxiety and insomnia. Instead, he asked me what I'd like to talk about.

I spoke about the heartbreak of watching my mother's strength and dignity being stripped away by her terminal illness. I spoke about watching her body shrink, her hair fall out, her skin becoming stretched over her skeletal frame and her life force eroding noticeably each and every day before my eyes.

I talked about the betrayal and anger I felt about my dad's affair, and the pressure of keeping his secret while the other woman, *my godmother*, was still very present in our lives – coming over most weekends, gifting my mother clothing from her wardrobe and presenting herself as a supportive family member during this trying time.

I spoke about the lack of support I felt from my sister, who, admittedly, was married and had three children to take care of, and yet put all the pressure on me. I was witnessing my mother's decay, having to interact with a father who I knew was only physically present, seeing my godmother regularly and having to constantly battle with the sheer perversion of it all. And I spoke about the instability I was facing in my acting career, despite the pockets of success I had enjoyed. I shared the very real fear I felt that the only predictable thing in my future was Mum's funeral. I definitely did not speak about being gay.

The psychologist wasn't concerned with any of what I had said. Instead of addressing or even acknowledging any of these issues, he launched into what felt like a rehearsed speech about his specialisation in hypnotherapy. He claimed he had successfully cured people through that practice from addictions to cigarettes and alcohol and – wait for it – homosexuality.

I wasn't a smoker or a drinker, nor did he feel the need to elaborate on those two. Instead, he fixated on the latter, and brought up countless stories of kids with 'same-sex attractions' being brought to him by their parents, of young priests in the seminary brought in by bishops who were concerned about their 'disordered' attraction to men, of monks, friars and nuns (oh my) who struggled with the same 'affliction'. All clients who he had been able to *help*.

It was obvious that his session with Mum beforehand had focused on one thing, and that he had been tasked with just one job: to hypnotise the gay out of me. The one thing that I hadn't brought up with him. The one thing I was least interested in talking to *him* about. I didn't say much at that point because I knew I had been lured into a trap. My back was against a wall, and the bars on my cage never felt more inescapable. He took my silence as licence and suggested that he start hypnotherapy on me straight away.

This was the first time in my life that I rejected the idea of changing myself. I'd spent years praying deeply each day that somehow a switch would be flicked and I'd start liking girls, years believing that I *was* wrong for being gay. I had never acted on my feelings and I had yearned on the deepest level possible to be changed. And yet, on this occasion, what I felt was insulted.

I was insulted that I hadn't been informed ahead of time that this was what I was there for. Insulted that the deep troubles I had poured my heart out about had been disregarded like used pieces of toilet paper. Insulted that the good person and dedicated son I had been didn't count for anything. And insulted that my personality and the achievements I had accomplished so far had boiled down to absolutely nothing. The 'gay' thing was all that mattered. All that my twenty-five years of life had come to was that I was gay, and it was the utmost priority for that to stop. With my mother's guaranteed death fast approaching, it was imperative for her to set me on the right path, once and for all.

It was a new feeling for me, to feel disgusted by the idea of being artificially altered, especially by a professional whose job it was to improve mental health, not further erode it. Allowing someone – a complete stranger, mind you – to put me in a vulnerable state and then penetrate my mind against my conscious wishes felt like psychological rape. And so, for the first time in my life, I went with my instincts. In my head, I made the decision to block out whatever it was that he was about to do.

He started with another prayer, and then played soothing sounds of waves lapping against the shore.

'Relax your whole body,' he said, 'and let yourself melt into the couch cushions.'

I sat back, trying to imitate relaxation while my body tensed up in defence.

'Close your eyes and try to visualise the sounds you're hearing. What does the beach look like? What kind of trees can you see? What colour is the water? Paint a picture of it in your mind and place yourself there.'

In spite of myself, a mental image did start to form.

'Let your mind drift into total relaxation and think about nothing except for the calm of the beach,' he continued.

It was a tougher job than I expected to resist what was happening. While I was resolute that I would not allow myself to be taken advantage of this way, in order to sell the performance of someone who was 'going with it', I did need to listen to his instructions and play the part. *Luckily,* I thought, *I'm an actor.* And yet I was terrified. In keeping an ear out for his prompts, I worried that there could be a possibility that it would work, and I would end up as nothing more than a puppet on his string.

It helped that he had a very thick accent and I struggled at times to understand what he was saying. He spoke of the love God has for us all, and of the beauty of heaven. He spoke of purity and the importance of biblical instruction, and of the harmful and seductive temptations of the devil. And he spoke of the fulfilment gained from overcoming sin. None of this felt like an unbiased third party whose aim was to aid me in the mental health issues I was currently experiencing.

It went on for about forty minutes, and as he prattled away I deliberately thought about literally anything else other than what he was saying. Thankfully, I never 'went under' and managed to stay in my own mind the whole time.

'And just stay like this for a moment and open your eyes whenever it feels right. Take your time.'

It was finally over. I waited for what I thought was a convincing amount of time and eventually opened my eyes. I pretended to him that I had just fallen asleep. He was quite pleased with that outcome, no doubt putting it down to another successful hypnotism that would undoubtedly have fruitful results in the long run. He then fossicked around in his paper metropolis for a bunch of printouts. One of them contained instructions on breathing exercises to assist with anxiety, while the rest of the stack was religious meditations. And then we ended the session as we had begun, with a prayer.

It was a quiet drive home. There was an elephant in the car that neither Mum nor I acknowledged. I concluded that I was simply unknown to the person I cared about the most, and that what she did know, she didn't like. I was so let down that she couldn't have just talked to me about it, that she felt it was better to trick me into a situation that I wasn't able to back out of. But that was just it – it was more important for her to change me than to connect with me.

Even though I had spent so many years *wanting* to change, everything about this first encounter with the psychologist, and the subsequent occasions when I saw him, felt intrusive, wrong and utterly disrespectful. 'Reductive' was not a term I had at hand back then, but that's what it was.

Despite those feelings, however, I continued to see him on a weekly basis, and kept up the act that the hypnotherapy was working while tuning him out each time. I only went because it was what Mum wanted. Given everything she was going through, I wanted to relieve her of any unnecessary worry, which, in my case, was that she would die having failed to raise a good, Catholic, *heterosexual* boy. This was one last thing I could do for her. I played the part of someone who was benefiting from the experience and provided glowing reviews of the help I was getting from him, to ease her mind.

CHAPTER EIGHT

Love and Loss

Over the next few months, my mission in life was to make sure that Mum was as comfortable as possible. I watched her lose more and more weight, I watched the little energy she had left drain from her body, and I saw the worry in her sunken eyes. While all of this was happening, and after rebutting any job offers that had come along since I wrapped filming on *Dance Academy*, I was offered a lead role in a film called *Forbidden Ground*. It was a short three-week commitment, shooting in a remote part of New South Wales. Though I had been reluctant to work during this time, the short timeframe was attractive, and it gave me an excuse to no longer be subjected to the weekly hypnotherapy sessions. So I accepted the offer.

From a creative standpoint, it was an opportunity to do something different after spending the past years playing a fairly low-stakes teenage love interest. I was twenty-six now, and was yearning for more complicated characters and storylines that challenged me. Playing an Irish World War I soldier trying to survive in no-man's-land was exceptionally different from anything I had done before. It was a gruelling shoot, mostly throughout the nights, that took a huge physical and emotional toll, but was very creatively fulfilling. However, when I returned from the shoot at the end of the three weeks, Mum's decline was severe. I was shocked when I saw her. She was gaunt. She barely had energy to turn her head, and she was no longer able to walk. This was right before Christmas, and Dad was quietly excited by the fact that we didn't have to decorate the house that year because, for once, we were no longer going to host our dozens of relatives for Christmas lunch.

Mum loved Christmas. It was her favourite time of year, and her joy and exuberance for it were infectious. Our yearly tradition was to decorate the house completely, make a Christmas pudding from scratch and, obviously, host the extended family. But this year, it was clear that this Christmas would be her last. Due to her legs no longer working, she was unable to make it down the stairs and was stuck alone in her room. I was heartbroken to see it. So one day while she was mercifully asleep, I secretly bought a bunch of decorations, borrowed a small tree from my best mate Dave and decorated her bedroom as she slept. I just wanted to bring her a little bit of joy, one last time.

When she woke, she called me to her room.

'Thank you, darling,' she said with a soft smile, unable to muster the energy to do or say much else. I sat and watched her favourite show, *Downton Abbey,* with her, but whenever I looked over, she was gazing at the humble ten-inch plastic

Christmas tree and the sparkling silver tinsel decorating her bedside table, her head tilted on a slight angle, a faraway look in her eyes. She knew she was about to die. I could see it in her eyes and that was a horrible thing to witness.

At about 1 am on 1 January 2012, Dad knocked on my door. Mum had collapsed while trying to use the commode beside her bed. He couldn't lift her up and needed my help. We rushed to her. She was propped up beside the bed, sitting in a puddle. The look of shame in her eyes when I reached her bedroom was devastating. She was humiliated to be seen this way. Cancer had stripped her of all dignity. Though she had become incredibly thin, she was a dead weight and it took several attempts for Dad and me to lift her up. We cleaned her and the carpet up, trying not to draw too much attention to it as she was mortified by what had happened. She couldn't make eye contact with me, but kept muttering, 'I'm sorry, George', her childhood pet name for me. A few hours later, in the morning, an ambulance arrived to take her into palliative care and she left our home for the last time. What a wonderful way to start a year.

Her room at the palliative care facility had a large glass door that overlooked a garden. Vines grew up the dark brick walls. In the centre of the perfectly manicured lawn was a little fountain that birds would come to and drink from. As far as deathbeds go, at least this one had a pretty view.

On 3 January, I was meant to fly down to Melbourne to take part in a four-day acting masterclass with a famed Hollywood acting coach whose clientele included Brad Pitt, Halle Berry and Charlize Theron. It was an exclusive masterclass based on audition, and only thirty actors from around the country had been selected to work with her, including Sarah Snook, now of *Succession* fame. It was a huge honour to have successfully auditioned for it and I had been rehearsing for weeks but I told Mum I was going to pull out. She wouldn't hear of it. She didn't want to take this opportunity away from me. Moreover, her doctors told me that their experience led them to believe that she still had a few weeks to live. So I packed my bags and headed to Melbourne. As I was at the airport, she called me to wish me luck.

'Do a good job. I love you,' she said. I didn't know it at the time, but those were the last words she would ever say to me.

The method of acting for this masterclass revolved around substituting real-life events and people into the scenes that you are performing in order to elicit the most genuine emotions. The scene I was performing was about saying goodbye to someone; with Mum's situation, my emotions were incredibly raw and my 'substitution' was strong.

On the morning of 4 January, the first scene was performed for the master acting coach. It was a scene from the movie *Warrior*. It was a highly emotional interaction between two brothers, and the two actors onstage gave incredibly moving performances. When they were done, the Hollywood acting coach took hold of a microphone and started grilling them about their scene preparation. One of the actors was asked what his 'substitution' was for achieving his emotions. He said that his ex had miscarried, and that he was substituting his miscarried child into the scene, apologising for not being able to save them. Heavy stuff. He was then questioned further and given feedback that his emotion had felt self-indulgent. The coach asked, 'You said it was your ex. So you're no longer together? Are you with anyone now? Do you have any kids?'

'Yeah,' he replied awkwardly. 'I'm married to someone else and we have a one-year-old.'

'Well, then,' said the acting coach. 'Fuck the dead one. You've replaced it!'

An audible gasp reverberated around the room as everyone sat in stunned silence. I looked down at my scene-prep notes and grew concerned that, given my current circumstances, I wouldn't be emotionally able to handle a critique like that. A few hours later, after several other scenes had been performed with similar critiques, I received a tap on the shoulder and was asked to step out of the theatre. My dad had tracked down the number for the acting school that was hosting the workshop and called to say that I needed to return to Sydney immediately. I was on the phone, standing in the foyer of the theatre with a man I had never met before. As my dad said those words to me, all I could think to say was, 'What does that mean?'

Dad simply replied, 'She's going.'

Instinctually, I grabbed the stranger standing with me and held onto him. I'm not a tactile person, and yet I've never held onto someone like that. He had no idea what was going on while I broke down, sobbing uncontrollably into his shoulder. He was lovely about it. He collected my things from the theatre, drove me to my hotel to grab my belongings and took me to the airport. I called Alicia Banit, who had played my 'sister' Kat on *Dance Academy*. We had grown as close as actual siblings during the two years of filming together and she stayed on the phone with me for hours. The first flight I could get on was at 7 pm. Those hours felt like an eternity. As the flight took off, I was barely able to stand the anxiety. I closed my eyes and said a little prayer to Mum. I asked her, if she was out there, to get me through the flight. I'm a notoriously bad sleeper and have never been able to sleep on a plane. And yet that night I fell into a deep sleep almost instantly, only awoken by the jolt of the wheels hitting the tarmac as we landed in Sydney. I switched my phone on to see if there were any updates and noticed that I had dozens of messages in my inbox. The top one was from one of my former teachers at Redfield. It read, *I am sorry for your loss. Praying for you.* The next message was from one of my cousins, reiterating the same.

Mum was gone. I had missed it. And I never got the chance to say goodbye.

Sitting in my seat with the plane taxiing toward our gate, I tried to keep it together. In the row in front, a young girl suddenly recognised me from *Dance Academy* and started begging her mum to get out her phone so she could take a photo with me. I've never been *that* guy, but in this moment I was. Though it was night-time and we were inside a well-lit aircraft, I put my sunglasses on, grabbed my things and marched my way up the aisle, pushing in front of everyone. I explained to the cabin crew what was happening, and they allowed me to wait at the front of the plane so I could be first to get off.

One of my other cousins was picking me up from the airport. I saw her waiting by baggage claim, her eyes red and swollen from tears like mine.

We picked up my bags and drove for over an hour to the palliative care facility where Mum had taken her final breath.

I hugged my sister and my dad, and we stood together at the foot of Mum's bed, where she was lying in repose. Though I wish I had been there, my sister told me that Mum had not been in her right mind for the last few hours of her life. Perhaps it was a blessing that I had been spared from seeing her that way. Lying on that bed, she looked the most peaceful I had seen her in years. Her time of death had been 7 pm – right when my plane took off and I sent her that little prayer asking for help. Mumma had my back.

When I got home, I thought that everything would come out. And yet I was surprised to discover that, when I closed my door, what I felt was relief. Mum was no longer in pain, and the worry of 'when' was now removed.

Though our worldviews were completely different, and I can't deny that she was responsible for many of the issues I had to deal with, I loved my mum deeply. She was still my mumma, and nothing could compare to the solace of her bear hugs. Despite everything that had transpired, I knew that she had only ever wanted the best for me, based on her own beliefs. She was a beautiful, pure person, and the world is at a deficit without her in it.

***

In the months prior to her death, Mum and Dad had decided to buy a smaller house for us to move into. She had chosen a place that was right around the corner from Tangara School for Girls because she loved her school so much. In the lead-up to the move, she painstakingly catalogued everything in our home – taking photos of each item and assigning colour-coded stickers to each of her siblings, which they then placed beside the items they claimed. She passed away a few weeks before the move was scheduled to happen, however. Although it had always been the plan that they would take the items before we moved, it was oddly comical to witness the parade of uncles and aunts coming for collection while we planned the funeral. While my dad, my sister and I picked out the flower arrangements, coffin and hymns for the ceremony, our home was being picked clean. Most of the items up for grabs were my grandmother's antiques that many of her children had been eyeing off their whole lives. Fights over Mum's catalogue ensued, with multiple aunts and uncles feeling they had more right to certain items than their siblings.

My grandmother was also upset at how we were planning the funeral. She had been placed in an aged-care facility in the months leading up to Mum's death, and she didn't like that she couldn't have more say in the funeral arrangements. I had made the decision that I wouldn't ask any of Mum's siblings to do readings at the ceremony. I have been to many funerals, and I always found it a little cruel to put people in such an emotional state up on the pulpit in front of everyone. My dad, my sister and I weren't taking part, either. Instead, we had cousins from our generation doing all the readings, making sure each family was represented. My grandmother saw this as an insult, but she was mostly worried about one son in particular. I soon received a phone call from that uncle, telling me he was offended that I hadn't asked him to be involved. When I told him that I thought he might cry while doing a reading, he said, 'Only people with no faith cry at funerals.' He cried at the funeral.

Over a thousand people came to Mum's funeral. The church was overflowing, with hundreds of people outside listening to the ceremony through speakers that had been set up. The kids from her school formed a guard of honour, which stretched for hundreds of metres down the street. It was a beautiful funeral and it was so heartwarming to see how many people's lives she had touched. She deserved it, and I'm thrilled that we were able to make it such a special day. I wouldn't have changed a thing – sorry, Uncle.

Mum's gravesite was right next to a busy main road. My little cousin, who has autism and is enthralled by death, was having the time of his life and reminded me several times, 'Your mum is in that coffin. It's going in the ground.' It was hard to hear the priest during that part of the service, among the rushing trucks and the loud pop music wafting from the car wash next door, but as she was lowered into the ground, a feeling of relief settled over me. For a moment, everything was still and quiet. 'Goodbye, Mum,' I whispered, and my little cousin squealed with excitement as the coffin disappeared from sight.

We held the wake in the hall of Tangara School for Girls, where she had taught for so many years. I knew Mum would have loved that. It was also convenient as we were expecting a lot of people and didn't want to deal with the clean-up at home. It wasn't until after the funeral was over that my emotions really took hold of me. Planning the funeral had kept her alive, somehow, and with so much to do in such a short period of time, there was never a moment to pause and take stock. But when it was over and Dad and I finally got back to our almost empty house, reality set in, and everything came spilling out. I wept, and I weep now writing this.

Though it does sadden me to say this, what has become clear over the years is that Mum had to die in order for me to live. If she hadn't gotten sick and was still alive, I'm not sure I would have ever come out. I had a mum who loved me so much that she wasn't thinking about the immediacy of the here and now of this earthly life. She was thinking about my eternal future, and her love for me meant that every choice she made for me was in determination of my place in eternal glory. I can't fault a person for wanting the absolute best for me for all eternity. And I recognise her efforts as being her ultimate expression of love for me. I cannot ever say that my mother didn't love me, as I had such proof of how far her love for me went, no matter how misguided her efforts were. And I loved her right back, with everything I had. We just couldn't be honest with each other.

It is a shame that I know how desperately disappointed she was about my sexuality, and that the last few months of her life were tarnished by the hypno/conversion therapy she subjected me to. To this day, when people say to me, 'Your mum would be so proud of you,' I can't agree with them because she died with me believing the opposite, and I won't ever get any closure on that. But what did become clear is that she was the main reason why I had always felt so trapped by my reality. She had always been the mouthpiece of Catholic purity in the home, and without her hypervigilant presence in my life, I started to feel the dawning of a freedom to finally figure myself out.

Her death, therefore, was the catalyst for my coming-out journey. However, I was completely unprepared for the world that I was about to step into.

CHAPTER NINE

Baby Steps

I stopped visiting the hypnotherapist once Mum had passed. I had only ever done it to make her happy. Therapy would have been sorely needed during this time, but not the Opus Dei kind of therapy.

It was a bleak twelve months after Mum died. Within days of her funeral, not only were Dad and I turfing family heirlooms into the trash, but Dad had also started to spend every evening having dinner with my godmother. She had extended the invite to me, too, but I couldn't think of anything worse than being a third wheel for my father and cousin/godmother.

Dad and I would spend the day throwing memory after memory into the giant bin outside, while at night I would be alone in an empty home while he dined with the woman he had been seeing behind my mother's back for years.

Dad had told my sister and me that anything we didn't want to keep of Mum's would be thrown away and, as my sister was incapable of going through any of it, the task fell on me to be the keeper of my mother's memory.

I pawed through her belongings, and eventually came across a stash of letters she had received during the 90s. It soon became obvious that these were the other side of her correspondence during our time in Ireland. It felt rude to read her private letters, but she was dead and I was in mourning. I wanted to feel some sort of connection with her, and invading her privacy at this time made me feel like I could understand her a little better. Through these letters, I learned how miserable she had been during our time in Ireland. She had hated our isolated life there, which was such a shame for me as I had loved it so much. The letters she had been receiving spoke about her duty to her husband, and also her duty to her family and how she had to stay strong. All the letters, including those from the priest who had been her spiritual advisor, encouraged her to return to Australia and be closer to her own family unit. I started to get the feeling that our trip to Australia during the Christmas of 1992 might have been somewhat planned. Perhaps she had never intended on returning to Ireland after that trip; maybe she had used her father's illness as an excuse to stay in Sydney, and my sister and me as ransom against my father, who had remained in Ireland for so long. The turmoil of that time made a bit more sense this way.

Given my knowledge of how manipulative, controlling and convincing my mother had been, I couldn't discount this possibility. And after losing pretty much all trust in the parents who had raised me, I honestly didn't know what to think. None of us had ever communicated properly, held back by the constant demands of perfection from the religious world we had lived in. But none of it was true. Our family dealt in secrecy, and reality had never mattered as long as the public perception matched how we were meant to be. But this revelation gave me much pause for thought, and it made me sad to think that my parents had broken my trust so much that I couldn't take them at face value. Maybe Mum *had* kidnapped my sister and me, and used us a way to get what *she* wanted. But maybe not. Who am I to really say, but I know that she did always get her own way and had used her manipulative trickery to force me into conversion therapy under false pretences.

After a couple of weeks of turning our family memories into trash, my dad and I moved into the tiny house that he and Mum had picked out prior to her death. It was just him and me now, and we barely saw or talked to one another.

Unfortunately, the time I had taken off work during the last months of Mum's life had left me completely broke. Mum had left no will, or none that I was privy to, so now I was out on my own. I took a job working at a wedding reception venue on weekends, playing piano during the cocktail hour, and I started working as a gym receptionist during the week. The second season of *Dance Academy* was due for release soon, and I was contractually obligated to film promotional videos for the show only a week after her funeral and paint a smile on my face while I did so. Meanwhile, I was still living with my father in this strange new house that didn't feel like home. We barely interacted, and he spent every night of the week at my godmother's house while I continued to turn a blind eye.

Without anything or anyone holding me back, my focus was on my future. I was also feeling more and more that I was probably going to do something gay soon. The religious hypocrisy that my father's relationship represented, along with the absence of my mum's constant and judgmental religious supervision, meant that I was sensing a freedom in myself that I had never experienced before. When guys caught my gaze in the gym mirror, I no longer looked away. Whenever I found myself in the Sydney CBD after an audition, I would deliberately park my car near Oxford Street and spend half an hour walking up and down it, just so I knew what it felt like to walk proudly along a street that was known for being 'gay'. I even started chatting online to men, though I used the fake name 'Brad Hayes' because I was still too scared for 'Tim Pocock' to actually be gay.

I was in grief, I was rebuilding my life, and I was starting to experiment with what it felt like to actually be me. The problem was that I still viewed my instincts as intrinsically and morally wrong, and so even though I felt certain that something gay was in my future, I wasn't at all comfortable with it.

A couple of months later, the second season of *Dance Academy* had its premiere in Sydney. Superfans and competition winners attended along with the cast and crew, and it was a lovely and wholesome distraction from the grief I had been going through. After the premiere, the producers and cast went out for celebratory drinks. I didn't join them, however. It took all my emotional energy to even attend the premiere and pose happily for pictures with the fans. I just wasn't ready for a big social function like that.

I took my leave and started walking through Sydney to catch a bus home. As I walked down George Street, a little ahead of me, I noticed a handsome man stepping out of a travel agency. He was wearing the organisation's uniform and was locking up the store for the day. As he turned his key in the lock, he looked up and we made eye contact. The sounds of the bustling street, car horns and sirens faded out. All I could hear was my heartbeat pulsating in my eardrums.

As I walked past him, I looked back and he was still staring at me. He unlocked the door and, with a nod of his head, beckoned for me to join him inside. My legs did the walking while my head screamed at me to stop. But I didn't. In a flash, I found myself standing awkwardly in the entrance to the store, with him ushering me into a back room. I didn't know what I was expecting. I honestly just wanted to kiss a man. He, however, had other things in mind. And soon he was thrusting something in my face that I had absolutely no idea what to do with. I felt responsible. I had given the wrong impression, and it was absolutely my fault for being in this situation; it was therefore my duty to at least go through with it and give him what he wanted. We never exchanged names or even said any words to each other, and when he was finished, I walked back out onto the street and had never felt worse about myself.

I was a couple of blocks away from St Patrick's Church Hill, a Catholic church in the CBD known for its almost hourly mass times and constant confession. With the smell of the man's cologne clinging to me and the wetness of his saliva around my mouth, I ran there as fast as I could. I needed to confess. I needed to purge my soul of this sin. I had just signed my contract with the devil and needed to make amends immediately. I was in total panic.

However, when I arrived at the church, they were in full swing with a wedding ceremony. The church was packed and there was no confession available. Perhaps this immense feeling of shame was meant to be my punishment. As I hailed a taxi to get me home as quickly as possible, I could only hope that I wouldn't die before I got a chance to make my reconciliation.

That wasn't, however, the first time I had experienced something like that. I'm sorry to reveal this now, but it is the right time. There had been one other time, when I was eighteen years old.

A male, someone I had been close to all my life and trusted, had been visiting our family. One night, when he and I were alone together, he kissed me. As a gay person who had never once acted on that compulsion, I was so repressed and curious that I initially went with it, until he started to thrust his penis in my mouth and wouldn't take no for an answer. Of course, I felt that all the blame lay with me and, even after I had finally pushed him off me and left the room, I felt that it was my fault for allowing him to kiss me in the first place, and for giving in to the temptation that was in front of me. Until now, only about two or three people know about this incident. The person involved is now married to a woman, and has kids, and I'm not about to ruin his life by naming names. But he knows who he is.

The experience with the random man at the travel agency played over and over in my head for months. And while it hadn't been a great experience, I also hadn't hated it. It was mostly regrettable because of my moral feelings toward it at the time. However, my understanding of 'morals' was also being tested. Dad became engaged to my godmother within months of my mum's death, and the hypocrisy of that made me feel more and more like I would soon allow gayness to be part of my future. Because, unlike him, my actions weren't coming at anyone else's expense.

I spent the rest of the year with my head down and saved up as much money as I could. Alongside my jobs at the wedding reception venue and gym, I also shot a film called *Lemon Tree Passage* in Adelaide. I played an American tourist in Australia who was interested in an urban myth about a section of road that had a deathly apparition associated with it. Based on a popular YouTube video that depicted a ghostly encounter while travelling down a remote road, the film depicted a fictionalised explanation for the paranormal activity that had been reported in the area. It was an opportunity to again do something different and, unlike the previous film I had shot, *Forbidden Ground*, the production actually paid its actors. It also gave me another excuse to leave the home I was sharing with my dad and continue to keep my career dreams alive.

As I was dealing with all these life changes and working as much as I could, I put every cent I was earning toward my next goal: returning to Hollywood and trying to take my acting career to the next level.

In January 2013, twelve months after my mum's passing, I used the fruits of my labour to return to Los Angeles, this time surrounded by the actor-friends I had made over the last few years. A large group of us shared a house in West Hollywood, including Jordan Rodrigues, Keiynan Lonsdale, Alicia Banit, Lincoln Lewis and Christian Antidormi. We were all there for the same purpose and we had each other's backs.

Unlike my previous stints in Los Angeles, this time I had multiple credits and a supportive group of friends, and didn't have to worry about any dying family members back home. The world felt full of possibility, and the newfound freedom I was experiencing made me feel not only like I could find the next progression of my career aspirations, but also that I would probably kiss another boy soon. But this time, I was determined for it to be a more positive experience, and on my own terms. I just had no idea how to go about it, and while I was excited by the idea, I was also terrified by it. I still hadn't come out to anyone and my sexuality still felt like a secret I had to keep.

The day after I arrived in Hollywood, I was immediately cast in a new TV series on NBC called *Camp*. I had taped my audition and sent it via email the day before I left for America and, like every audition, expected to hear nothing back. And yet, on this occasion, I was successful. I would be playing one of the lead roles in a comedy series about a failing summer camp run by a woman played by none other than Oscar-nominated, Golden-Globe-winning Australian icon Rachel Griffiths. Though the show was set in America, it was a co-production with an Australian company and therefore filled with Australian cast (because we're cheaper than Americans, and just grateful to have the work), and it was being shot in Queensland. It was another irony that I had set my sights on leaving Australia behind to pursue my American acting career and yet, within hours of landing in Hollywood, found out that I would be returning to home soil. But it was on a big network, with producers from *Gossip Girl* and *Deception,* so it represented a huge jump in my career, especially after the last couple of years I had been through.

Camp wasn't due to commence production for several months and I had already paid for a few months' accommodation in LA, so I figured I would just stay and have a bit of a break. After all the trials and heartbreak of the last few years, I felt that I deserved this moment to just live my own fucking life. And that is when I met Sam.

Sam was a gay friend of a friend. He was a ruggedly handsome, horse-riding cowboy, and my attraction to him was instant. He was Australian, too, but wasn't in LA to audition like the rest of us. He was there for a vacation and, now that I had been cast in something and was therefore not able to audition for anything else, I had the same amount of time on my hands as he did, so we started to hang out. One night, he invited me to join him for drinks at a sports bar on Santa Monica Boulevard in West Hollywood, the gay mecca of LA. It was my first time being in an all-gay environment and I was equal parts excited and petrified. But after a few hours, and bolstered by liquid courage, I plucked up enough daring to tell him that I had a crush on him. We kissed, and it was another first for me – kissing someone who I actually wanted to kiss.

Sadly, due to my naivety, kissing him made me feel like he now *had* to be my boyfriend. Why would he kiss me if he wasn't interested? While the questions in my brain spun out of control, I trotted drunkenly after him as he led me back to the apartment he was renting. I didn't know what to do in the bedroom. After some very awkward fumbling, we both fell asleep in the early hours of the morning. But in my naive mind, I had just met my life partner. This was a huge risk for me and, after so many years of hearing about how people only become intimate once they are sworn together for life, this represented a huge life decision for me. *Good grief, Tim, how much you still had to learn.*

After an awkward parting the next morning, I didn't hear from him for over a week, despite me texting him constantly like a lovesick teenage desperado. I pined over him and felt like I had taken this life-changing risk only for it to have meant absolutely nothing to him. I couldn't concentrate on anything else. My upcoming role no longer meant anything to me. I had made myself more vulnerable than I had ever done before, and it had meant nothing. *I* meant nothing. My sheltered brain simply couldn't comprehend that sometimes a kiss was just a kiss. Internally, I felt that I had compromised everything I had shown so much discipline against, and I regretted my actions. This deep misery was God's vengeance toward the evil that I had done. And I had no-one to turn to. I wasn't 'out' to anyone in my life and I knew that my family would never understand. So I kept it to myself, like I had always done.

However, after almost two weeks, Sam finally wrote back to me. He told me he loved spending time with me and wanted to see me again. He asked me to join him at a gay club that very night. I was a lovesick puppy and completely disregarded the days of being ignored by him. I was overjoyed that he wanted to hang out again. I cancelled my plans with my friends without giving a reason why and, in secret, drove back to the West Hollywood gay strip to meet up with him.

We went to a bar called Rasputin. Another first – my first time in a gay nightclub. This place was something else. It was the very antithesis of the sheltered environment I had grown up in. We walked into a bar area with glass flooring, under which lay actual humans dressed in lingerie waving at the people walking on top of them. One of the glass chambers even had a live snake writhing around in it. We then walked down to the dance floor. The space was filled with gyrating shirtless bodies, abs and pecs as far as the eye could see, illuminated by strobe lighting and lasers. Smoke machines went off at intermittent intervals and the bass beat perforated my eardrums. This was not my scene. I was used to ornate churches, stained glass windows and Gregorian chants reverberating through the halls. This couldn't be more different – but I was determined to step outside my comfort zone.

I was also only there for Sam, to spend more time with the guy who I had been pining over for days.

It wasn't long before Sam flirted his way into getting us invited to a VIP table with a group of much older men, who were more than happy to have two young Australian pretty boys in their company. They plied us with liquor, and their hands went everywhere. While I wasn't comfortable with this, my inner monologue was repeating a similar refrain: it was my fault for giving the wrong impression, and I had no choice but to simply go with it. Next thing I knew, Sam had disappeared onto the dance floor with some other guy, leaving me alone with the gropey older men. The music deafened me, the flashing lights blinded me, and the smell of alcohol and sweat filled my nostrils. I hated this place. I no longer wanted to be there, but I had driven and had since been drinking, so how was I meant to get home?

I scoured the room for exits and noticed a guy on the dance floor staring directly at me. He was a very attractive man, with a handsome face and lean, muscular body. He smiled at me but I looked away. However, curiosity got the better of me. I kept looking back at him and, each time, he was not only still staring at me but also moving gradually closer with each glance. I felt like I was in a nightmare of my own making and was completely overwhelmed. I needed an escape.

I decided to hide in the toilet, which had always been my safe place. Perhaps I'd hear from Sam, or perhaps I could figure out a way of getting home. I just needed to get away from these men and their roaming hands. I pushed my way through the sweaty dance floor in what I thought was the direction of the bathrooms. All of a sudden, a hand grabbed mine. It was the guy who had been staring at me. He pulled me through the sea of man flesh to an area with a little more space. I thanked him but said I was just looking for the bathroom. He showed me where it was and said he would wait for me.

I spent what felt like an age in that toilet cubicle. Drunk and high partiers were banging on the door for me to come out, but I was used to that from my school days. Eventually, I emerged and found that the guy had indeed waited for me the entire time. He had purchased us a few drinks and said he wanted to get to know me.

I didn't want to be rude, since he had been so chivalrous as to buy me a drink, so we talked for a few minutes. As we did, I awkwardly sucked down the drink he had gotten for me. Soon, however, the room started to spin and my words weren't coming out of my mouth the way I intended. Though I had been drinking, it wasn't enough to have gotten me *that* drunk. Almost as soon as that realisation occurred to me, my legs started to feel like jelly.

I don't remember the rest of our conversation. I don't remember leaving the club. I don't remember agreeing to leave with him. I remember walking through the parking lot as he dragged me to his car. I remember that his car was yellow. I don't remember getting inside. I don't remember the car ride, apart from the world whizzing past me in a blurred haze. I don't remember walking into his house.

The next thing I do remember was the ceiling fan above me while I was flat on my back, naked in his bed. My clothes had been removed and I remember him trying to put things inside me that I didn't want. I remember feeling conscious but not able to express myself – like I was viewing what was going on as a third person. I remember trying to protest, but only gibberish coming out, and I remember him laughing at that. I remember that he had a red lamp beside the bed. As he continued to play with my body against my will, all I could focus on was that the ceiling fan above me was going so slowly that it might as well have not been on at all. After some time, I somehow found my voice and told him I needed to use the bathroom again. He was annoyed with me but pointed to the bathroom door in the hallway.

I walked unsteadily toward the door. My clothes were strewn across the floor and I had no memory of how that had happened. I kicked them toward the hallway outside the bedroom while he was looking the other way. When I got to the door, I grabbed them from the floor, found the front door and ran out into the streets of wherever I was, stark-naked. I sprinted up the road until I found a back alley. I slumped to the ground, exhausted, and fumbled with my clothes, trying to hide my naked body. In the near distance, I could hear him screaming into the night, 'Come back here, you little slut!'

I spent a long time in that dark, dingy alley, fading in and out of consciousness. Eventually, I managed to get to my feet.

I found a main road and hailed a taxi to take me back to my apartment.

The scariest thing is that literally no-one in the world knew where I was that night. My family was on the other side of the world, and wouldn't have approved of what I was doing. I hadn't been honest with my friends because I needed to keep my secret from everyone. As bad as it already was, it could have been a whole lot worse and no-one would have known.

The next morning, I knocked on Alicia Banit's bedroom door and asked her to talk. She had been there for me throughout my mum's illness and had always been a huge support and comfort to me during the toughest of times. After holding onto my secret for twenty-seven years, the events of the past week, and specifically the previous night, were too much for me to keep to myself.

Though I was no longer under the influence of whatever that guy had put in my drink, the words 'I'm gay' just wouldn't come out of my mouth. It felt like I had swallowed a whole watermelon that had lodged itself in my throat and made it impossible for the words to surface. I started shaking and crying uncontrollably.

Alicia went pale. 'Tim. You're scaring me.'

Eventually, with a blanket pulled over my face so I couldn't make eye contact with her, I managed to tell her the secret I had held onto my whole life.

'I … ' I stuttered.

'What?' she asked, sounding terrified.

'I ... I'm ... gay.' It winded me to say it, and I wailed uncontrollably.

She could not have been more beautiful in how she responded. She hugged me and didn't let go for a long time while I sobbed into the blanket. I had never fully appreciated the weight of the guilt that I had carried or how much of a burden it had been to hide it. Finally saying the words out loud was the most profound thing I had ever experienced.

Alicia slowly removed the blanket from my face and looked at me. Very gently, she said, 'You know I already knew, right?'

'Really?'

She gave me kind smile. 'I mean, it was kinda obvious.'

Finally, it was out there, and the relief I felt was like nothing I had ever experienced. The lead weight that had been chained around my soul for almost thirty years was suddenly gone. And now I wouldn't have to cope with the experiences of the previous night alone.

I didn't tell anyone else. Alicia and I kept it between us. She did tell me that what had happened to me was horrendous and that I shouldn't shoulder any blame for it. I was unconvinced of that, though, because, as a Catholic, I had been taught that if I put myself in a position of potential sin, then it *was* my fault and still counted as a sin. Rape was just as much the fault of the victim as the perpetrator, because the victim should never have been in that situation in the first place. I had gone to that club, I had drunk those drinks, I had spoken to that guy. If I hadn't succumbed to

Satan's temptation by accepting Sam's invitation, then none of it would have happened. Though it was a relief to finally be completely honest with someone for the first time in my life, I couldn't shake the guilt I was feeling.

Alicia spent the next few weeks trying to build my confidence and comfort with the idea of being gay. I feel so blessed that she was the person I came out to first. I will never forget that moment and will forever be grateful for the dignity and respect with which she treated me. Thanks, sis, I love you!

Shortly after that, I left LA to start shooting the TV series *Camp*. My character in the show was the 'hot, shirtless jock guy' trope, which honestly was quite a compliment to me since I had struggled with my weight and didn't think anyone in my acting classes over the years, let alone my family, had ever thought I could play that type of role. But he was kind of one-dimensional. Though he had a bit of a backstory, it wasn't enough to make him more than just eye candy on the show, and he was straight, so I needed to be as straight and 'hot' as I could possibly be. The film and TV industry at the time purported to be progressive, and yet a casting director had once told me that I shouldn't wear certain colours during auditions because they come across as gay. My agent had also told me that gay, or *gay-seeming*, actors would never play leading men or superheroes. Well, I'd already played leading men, and had played a superhero in *X-Men Origins: Wolverine*, so the joke was on them. Oh, and was it just me or did Troye Sivan play young Wolverine in that same movie? We gays had sneaked our way into the superhero world, under everyone's noses. But I can't deny that this was because our true identities were still under wraps at the time. Had they not been, maybe we wouldn't have been cast.

That being said, and after my recent experiences and explorations, I was constantly paranoid on the shoot of *Camp* that I would be fired at any moment due to my sexuality. It still had to remain hidden. The shoot went for five months, and the cast was coincidentally filled with a bunch of my former *Dance Academy* cast mates, including Dena Kaplan, Thom Green, Jordan Rodrigues and Isabel Durant.

It was a gorgeous experience to film this show with so many of my best friends while living in a resort hotel for months, and our shooting location, though incredibly remote and requiring a two-hour drive every day from our accommodation, was stunning. But I was preoccupied with all the recent changes in my personal life, and with how they would affect my career. Sam still messaged me from time to time, and though I hadn't appreciated how things had gone between us, I still, stupidly, gave him the time of day. He knew I was someone he could always get an ego boost from, and he milked that for all it was worth. It was a constant cycle of him pulling me in when he needed me, and pushing me away when I got too intense. And, yeah, I'll admit that I probably did come across as a bit intense, because I had no frame of reference for how gay dudes interacted with each other. I had also never really dated before, so it didn't matter that I was twenty-seven – I had the experience of a thirteen-year-old, and that was how it all made me feel. I did realise soon, however, that he really just needed a friend. Meanwhile, I was all about locking him down, clinging on to my teenage infatuation with him. I can laugh about it now, but honestly it was just stupid, stupid, stupid!

While I was filming *Camp*, Dad and my godmother got married. He asked me to be his best man. It was an awkward moment.

'Oh. Did you want to ask one of your brothers?' I replied.

'They've already had a turn,' he said. Charming.

So, in the interest of keeping the peace, I begrudgingly accepted. My feeling was, if they could go off and live their lives, I should be free to do the same thing. If they were allowed to be happy, then why not me too?

The day they got married was dramatic. Would you expect any less from me at this point?

I had told the *Camp* production company, well before the shoot had even started, that I wouldn't be available to work that day, as I was the best man at my father's wedding. The event was on a Saturday, and we shot Monday to Friday with weekends off, so it shouldn't have been a problem. However, the episode of the show we had been filming had gone way over the production schedule, and there was no way out of shooting a few scenes on the very day of the wedding. The ceremony was in Sydney, mind you, and I was in Queensland. So the compromise made by the show was that I would film these two scenes from 4 am in the morning (meaning a 1.30 am wake-up), so I could be on a plane back to Sydney in time for the afternoon wedding. One of those scenes was a sex scene, with my love interest played by the beautiful Dena Kaplan. The weather was atrocious, and Dena and I found ourselves wearing nothing but modesty patches in the pouring rain at 4 am and shooting an intimate moment surrounded by a crew we barely knew, as union laws prohibited our usual crew members from working overtime on a weekend. After completing the scenes, I was driven the several hours back from our remote location to the airport but, due to the weather, the flight was delayed. I landed in Sydney about fifteen minutes before the wedding was meant to start. The plan was that I would arrive at the hotel Dad was staying in, get ready with him and head to the church with the groom. Instead, I changed into my suit in the ammonia-scented public toilets at Sydney Airport and got a cab to the church – ironically, it was at St Patrick's Church Hill, which you'll recall from my blunder with the travel-agency guy a year earlier. I arrived as the bride was already walking down the aisle. I sprinted past her, and the priest celebrating the wedding (the same priest who had buried my mum twelve months prior) threw the ring box to me. I was panting and spluttering throughout the ceremony.

The reception was held at a swanky Sydney CBD hotel, where my uncle – my mother's brother – was the general manager. Some of Mum's other siblings were also invited to the wedding, which seemed odd to me. Surely they sensed how bizarre this situation was. Their recently deceased sister's husband was now marrying their cousin ... a bit out of the ordinary, no?

I hadn't eaten all day and so, when one of my uncles handed me a beer, it went straight to my head. Without being asked, or having prepared anything, I suddenly found myself on my feet giving a speech at the reception. I felt the room tense up a little as I started speaking off the cuff.

I opened with, 'A year ago, Mum died.'

Shit, Tim, pull it back, pull it back …

'Obviously, my sister and I have been worried about Dad ever since. I'm so grateful that Dad has found someone to take care of him and keep him company. So, to my new mum, welcome to the family.'

Okay, good save! Except I continued …

'Well, I guess you already were part of the family, since you're our cousin and you're also my godmother.'

Well, fuck.

Thankfully, it all seemed to go over everyone's heads, and my 'new mum' thanked me with tears in her eyes for my lovely words.

I flew back to Queensland the next day to continue filming. Though I spent the next several months expecting to be replaced or written out because I wasn't *straight* enough, I managed to keep the job to the end. It was a lovely shoot, despite being a time of great mental stress. I had so many things on my mind. By the end, I was utterly exhausted. I had signed a seven-year contract with the show and, as we left the set for the last time when we wrapped, I wondered if I really wanted this for the next almost-decade. However, it was a great opportunity for the future of my career and I couldn't deny that.

A week after we finished filming, I returned to Los Angeles. I had arranged a one-bedroom apartment for myself in Hollywood and was eager to make the most of the exposure that being a lead on a new American TV series might offer.

I started to train five days a week with a celebrity personal trainer in Beverly Hills, whose other clients included Emilia Clarke, Jessica Simpson and Kristin Chenoweth. Kristin's and Emilia's sessions often overlapped with mine, and I told Emilia that we must have met previously as she looked so familiar. She smiled and said, 'I would have remembered such a handsome face.'

I hadn't yet watched *Game of Thrones* but was mortified when a short while later, on my way home, I spotted a giant *Game of Thrones* billboard on Sunset Boulevard with her face staring down at me.

Kristin and I ended up having a lot in common. She was as charming and delightful as you would think, and when she had her debut performance at the Hollywood Bowl, she kindly gifted me tickets to her show.

It all sounds very 'Hollywood', and it really was a very 'Hollywood' period in my life. I was auditioning for, and getting close to, parts on big projects that could have been life-changing. I was being invited to network parties and rubbing shoulders with people who acted in some of my favourite TV series. On the evening of the NBC pre-Emmys party, I suddenly found myself in a conversation circle with the cast of *30 Rock*. It was everything I had worked for. I just needed to keep the momentum going and solidify my place in the industry.

It was during this time that I met a celebrity crush of mine. He was such an incredibly beautiful man and, after years of secretly drooling over him on my TV screen, he was suddenly flirting with me. One night, he came over to my apartment to watch *The Lord of the Rings*, as we had bonded over being absolute nerds for the trilogy. Halfway through the first film, I excused myself to use the bathroom. When I came back, he was no longer on the couch. I heard him call for me from my bedroom and discovered him naked in my bed. He simply said, 'I want to give you something.' I was twenty-seven, and that was how I punched my V-card.

I retreated to the bathroom afterward to process my feelings. On one hand, I had just had one of the most amazing experiences in my life, something that I had constantly imagined but never thought would actually happen. Not to mention the fact that it had happened with a celebrity crush. On the other hand, I was filled with shame and regret. After clinging onto my virginity and swearing my whole life that I would never submit to sinful temptation, it was now done and there was no turning back. But I felt good! But I also felt terrible? It was confusing and my brain was spinning around in my skull like a washing machine on a fast cycle.

Not wanting to leave him alone for too long, I ventured out of the bathroom only to find him trying to sneak out my front door without saying goodbye. When he realised he had been caught, he said that he had a big day coming up and needed to get home. He gave me a half-hearted kiss, and the door closed. I was left with my churning feelings, and empty beer bottles to clean up that only reminded me of what had just happened. I later found out that he was engaged and had cheated on his boyfriend with me. So much for those positive gay experiences I was looking for.

The demons started to do their work, telling me that this was to be expected for living such a sinful lifestyle. I had always been told there was no real satisfaction or fulfilment in giving in to the desires of the flesh, and it seemed this was true. I started to go back to daily mass again, praying to God that he would understand the dilemma I was facing and asking him to not just forgive me, but allow me to find happiness and peace in who I actually was. Alicia was no longer living in Los Angeles, and I hadn't told a single other soul, so I was back to keeping secrets and living with the turmoil inside my head alone.

A few weeks later, Sam returned to LA. He asked to spend a few days with me while he sorted out his accommodation and, like an idiot, I agreed. By then, I had made up my mind that he was a waste of my time and so I laid ground rules for him. One of which being that I didn't want him inviting other men back to my apartment. Not because I wanted him all to myself, but because I wanted him to respect my space.

He broke that rule. I discovered one day that he was using my iPad to log into his Facebook account and invite random men over to my apartment while I was out. When I found this out, I knew I had to have a chat with him.

However, on that particular day, he was out on a date with a guy called Liam who he had met online. It was Liam's birthday and they wanted to come back to my apartment for a swim. Being a good host and figuring that we would have the conversation the following day, I went out and bought some booze and a birthday cake for this Liam guy.

The three of us splashed around in the pool, drank and had a birthday celebration in my apartment. As the evening went on, Liam began to get very flirty with me and, eventually, Sam got upset. World War III broke out, with Sam accusing me of being disrespectful, to which I aired out all the dirty laundry of disrespect I had received from him for months. He grabbed his belongings and slammed the door on his way out, leaving birthday boy Liam and me alone together. I had been 'out' for all of two seconds and was already embroiled in such typical gay drama. Liam spent the night, though no funny business took place.

The following morning, Liam and I laughed about the night before and got breakfast together. I was completely charmed by him. He was a charismatic man with a very pretty face, a great sense of style, and similar dreams and aspirations to me. He had a beautiful singing voice and played me some of his demo tracks. I found myself connecting with him almost instantly and, unlike with my previous crushes, his interest seemed to match mine.

Over the next few weeks, we became inseparable. We shared a sense of humour, felt an undeniable attraction for each other and got along easily. He drove a Jaguar, which was his pride and joy, and though I'm not the superficial type who places importance on those things, it was an indication that he had his shit together. One thing I did notice, though, was that he never invited me back to his place.

In October, right around my twenty-eighth birthday, I was due to return to Australia to spend a few months consolidating my savings by getting a part-time job so that I could save enough to upgrade my US visa and make the move there permanent. I felt that Sydney didn't have anything to offer me in the long term; I had more friends living in LA than I did back home, and far more career opportunities there. With Dad now in a marriage I didn't approve of, and my sister busy with four children, it just made sense to give Hollywood a good, hard crack. Though this had been the plan all along, when the time came to return to Australia, I now had a boyfriend for the first time ever and had slowly started to come out to more and more of my friend group and had introduced them to Liam. I considered myself in love. Armed with the confidence that gave me, I was determined to come out to my family once back in Australia.

Dad and his wife took me out for my birthday, and I used the opportunity to tell them.

'So, you know my friend Liam in LA, who I told you about?' I said.

'Yeah, the singer, right?' replied my dad, barely glancing up from his food.

'Yeah.' I paused. 'Well, turns out he's more than just a friend.' I left that statement hanging in the air.

'Oh, so you're gay,' said my godmother, incredibly casually, like I had just told them that I liked eating chocolate.

'Right, I see.' Dad didn't sound the least bit surprised. And then we continued our dinner as normal.

I was relieved that they took it so well, but honestly their opinion didn't matter to me as I wasn't exactly in love with some of the moral choices they had recently made in their lives. I did, however, appreciate the fact that my godmother/stepmother made an effort to ask me questions about Liam and show an interest in our newfound relationship. Dad had not said much about it, but later in the evening, after they had driven home, my godmother called me.

'I know your father didn't say much tonight. He said that he didn't really want this for you, but was glad that you're happy.'

The next day, I told my sister.

I loved my sister dearly. We had always gotten along, apart from the standard teenage sibling spats from time to time, and shared the same sense of humour. I was her firstborn's godfather and I love her kids as if they were my own. I would often offer to babysit, not just to give her a helping hand, but more so because I genuinely loved spending time with my nieces and nephews.

I knew that she had been raised with the same strict conservative values as me, and her husband was also a Redfield boy with all the beliefs and biases that the school promoted. But she had always been my confidante. She knew the care I had given our mother when she herself had been unable to due to her own family responsibilities. She knew the secret I had been keeping for our father. She had watched me build my acting career on my own. And with so much change in our family in the eighteen months since Mum had died, I hoped that what I perceived as a close bond between us would be enough for her to understand, appreciate and empathise with my honesty.

I told her the same way I had told Dad and his wife.

'My friend Liam is more than just a friend.'

'Oh,' she said. 'I didn't realise you were ...' She trailed off.

'Really?' I replied. 'Seems like everyone I've told so far already knew.'

She contemplated this for a moment. 'Well, my husband and I were at a wedding the other week and we sat next to a gay guy at the reception. He was *actually* really nice.' She said with an air of surprise, because *obviously* we're all serial killers.

She didn't say much else on the subject, but it seemed, so far, that she had taken the news fairly well.

The very next day, the accommodation I had arranged in Australia fell through. I found myself suddenly stranded in Sydney with no place to call home. For obvious reasons, I didn't want to stay with my dad and his wife, so I called my sister to ask if I could crash on her couch for a few days while I figured out an alternative living situation. She, however, refused.

After my confession to her, she had told her husband. He and his brother were both perfect representatives of Redfield's extreme homophobic culture. Together with their dad, they had always been vocal in their opinions, constantly talking about gays as 'degenerates' and how much they hated them. I couldn't say that I was surprised that he hadn't been thrilled to hear about me, but I was surprised that my sister had not only told him, but also hadn't stood up for me. It wasn't her secret to tell, and I didn't think that my private chat with her had any relevance to her marriage. I had expected her to have my back.

The years of love between us, and the close connection that I thought we shared, seemed to have been erased overnight. The words she used were, 'My husband and I just wouldn't be comfortable with you under our roof.' When I challenged that, she added, 'We're trying to raise good Catholic children,' like I was planning to host a satanic ritual in their living room, brainwash the kids into worshipping demons and encourage them to all be gay too.

This was the very kind of reaction that I had anticipated my whole life and had prevented me from ever being honest in the past. This kind of reaction keeps innocent and lonely people from being honest with their loved ones. We risk losing everyone we love because of a simple fact about ourselves that they don't understand and refuse to try to. It honestly broke my heart.

With no other immediate option at hand, I had no choice but to ask Dad to stay with them, which was a scenario that I hadn't wanted to contemplate. It was an awkward situation and I felt so betrayed, alone and lost.

Two days later, my sister invited my dad and his wife over for lunch and extended the invitation to me – I guessed it was okay to be under their roof if it was for a condensed period of time and under strict supervision. When we arrived at their house, my sister's father-in-law was there. He was a man with a big personality and very strong opinions. At one point, at the lunch table in front of me as well as his grandchildren, he made the comment, 'All the Muslims and homosexuals should be rounded up and shot.' Everyone just laughed. I made eye contact with my sister and we shared a look. I knew she knew that what had been said was extremely offensive. I knew she knew that me being gay was only one per cent of who I was as a person, and that she knew the other ninety-nine per cent fully. But that was just the world we lived in, and I had to make peace with the fact that, through no fault of my own, that world was toxic. I went outside to play games with my nieces and nephews. I had a feeling it was probably the last time I'd get to see them for a while. The last few days had made me feel so unwelcome in my own home town that I wanted to escape back to where my friends were, where my career opportunities were, where I felt a comfort in my real identity and where my shiny new boyfriend was. I no longer belonged in my family. I belonged more in LA.

I called Liam and told him everything. He supported my decision to return to the States. The problem was that I had given up the lease on my LA apartment. Some of my furniture had gone to my best friends Dave and Russ, who had also just moved there, and I had given the rest of the furniture to Liam to look after. I had obviously planned to reclaim the furniture once I had returned to Los Angeles a few months later, when I'd get my own place, but now that I was making this new plan unexpectedly, and without having a chance to line anything up, Liam suggested that I just move in with him. We had only known each other for a handful of weeks and I had never even set foot in his apartment. I didn't even really know what he did for work. All I knew was that I felt unloved and unwanted where I was, and I needed to fill that void. So I made a reckless decision. I bought a ticket back to LA and the next day boarded the plane and left the events of the past few days behind me.

It was a fourteen-hour journey between Sydney and LA and I got no sleep while I contemplated how things had reached this point. I had been such a good Catholic boy all my life, had sworn against homosexuality and vowed that I would never give in to my 'same-sex attractions'. I had been the altar-serving, Sunday-mass-organ-playing, children's-choir-leading example of Catholic conservatism. And yet, in just a few months, I'd had a bunch of regrettable experiences, lost my virginity to a man and was now about to move in with my boyfriend to 'live in sin'. It was so far removed from any future I had ever pictured, and I felt that I was becoming everything I had said I would never be. Aside from feeling disconnected from my family, I felt disconnected from myself. As the plane flew through the night sky, all I could think was, *Who even am I?*

CHAPTER TEN

Call Me by What Name?

The name on my birth certificate is David Wallace. I was born on 24 October 1985 in Johannesburg, South Africa. My biological mother was a teenager who had already given birth to another son two years before I was born. Her parents had adopted the child as their own, and he was raised as her brother rather than her son. When my biological mother discovered that she was pregnant with me, she hid it from her family, as she didn't want to put any additional pressure on them, as well as whoever my father was. The day that she went into labour, she took herself to the hospital. Once I had arrived, she Irish-goodbye'd and I, David Wallace, became an orphan.

My actual parents are Australian but moved to South Africa in the eighties to adopt, as they had found it impossible to conceive. Adoption in Australia was, and remains, incredibly difficult, so they had moved to South Africa in order to become parents. They adopted my sister four years before I came along. As my biological mother hadn't registered me as a child for adoption while she was pregnant, I was a last-minute addition to the system and my parents received a surprise phone call saying that a child had suddenly become available.

Adoption is such a luck-of-the-draw situation. I could have been given to anyone. It was chance that determined that David Wallace would become Tim Pocock and everything that entailed. I'm ashamed to admit that there have been times where I have indulged in imagining an alternate scenario, where I was adopted by a couple who wouldn't have been fazed that the mysterious stranger they took into their home was actually gay. Parents who would have recognised this stranger's creative passions and allowed them to thrive, rather than repress them. Parents who could have been relied on to support this stranger's internal struggles and been there for him when he hit times of trouble. But at no point did this mean that my family didn't love me, or that I didn't love them. I know they did, and my love for them can't be questioned. However, their love came from a very specific understanding of what family meant, and of how their own family should look to the people around them. Their children needed to be a reflection of their own ideals and, therefore, my sister and I needed to meet those expectations. And if we didn't, it was their duty to mould us in the image that they felt was acceptable.

The adoption was never kept a secret from me; I've always known about it. I don't remember a specific moment when I was told I was adopted. But I do remember, with great fondness, that when I was very little, my mum would often call me her 'special little adopted boy' while covering me in kisses. I'm sure there must have been a day when I asked her what that meant because I can't remember a time when I *didn't* know what it meant. I really appreciate that I've always known. If anything, it made me feel more wanted, because my parents had to get visas, find work in a foreign country and jump through incredible hoops in order to call me their son.

Having said that, from a very early age there was always a sense that I had to be eternally grateful that I was given this opportunity in life. From birth, I was indebted to these people for taking me in, putting clothes on my back and a roof over my head, and educating me. Whenever I felt that my own individual interests didn't align with what they were trying to shape me into being, I felt a need to keep quiet because it would seem so ungrateful to show dissent, when they were responsible for everything that I had in my life. I could just as easily have not been adopted and remained in an orphanage, without any of the privileges that my adoption provided me. For that reason, it felt important to be a model child and the person they wanted me to be. My religious faith, therefore, became a way to prove my loyalty not only to God, but also to them.

It's only since seeking professional help from therapists that I've been able to unpack the abandonment issues that my adoption had subconsciously caused, and why that meant I was constantly betraying my own individuality by being a people pleaser, and therefore needing to present myself as what *others* wanted me to be as opposed to my true nature.

While I was filming the first season of *Dance Academy*, my sister's biological mum hired a private investigator to track her down. One night, my mum received a surprise phone call from her old neighbour in South Africa. The private investigator had found them and asked if they could get in touch with my parents. My sister didn't live with us anymore, as she was already married, and Mum wasn't inclined to share this news with her. Though I had never considered the situation before, in that instant I was certain that it wasn't Mum's choice to make. I told her that if she didn't tell my sister, I would. It was my sister's right to either accept or deny the request.

A few months later, my sister's biological mum landed in Sydney and spent two weeks living with us and getting to know her daughter. The resemblance between them was uncanny. Not only was my sister a carbon copy of her mum, but they had the same personality, sense of humour and even the same laugh.

It was interesting to witness this. I had never thought about the fact that there might be a family out there who looked like me, and who might have the same passions and drives, personality or sense of humour, and potentially the ability to understand me.

This chain of events led my parents to show me a document from the South African welfare office about my adoption, which contained information about my birth mother, her family and her situation at the time of my birth. It turns out she was musically gifted. I smiled when I read that. It was nice to know where I got it from, and I liked that she and I had that connection. I wondered what she would think if she knew what I had done with my life.

The background report about me mentioned that I had a brother, and even went so far as to say his name – we'll call him 'Kyle'. My father and I never had the closest of bonds, so a big part of me subconsciously yearned to have an older male figure in my life who I could relate to. Facebook was all the rage at the time and I figured there was a high chance that I would be able to find him. I did a search and limited the results to South Africa. Four results for that name came back. All but one of them were the wrong age. And the guy who was the right age had a square jawline, very blue eyes and – in some photos – honestly could have been me.

After a few weeks mulling it over, I eventually sent him a message. I asked him if he was related to the woman named in my background report. A day later, he replied that he was and questioned why I was asking. I told him we could be related. To me, it was entirely possible that he never knew about his own adoption and that I could be opening an entire can of worms for him by revealing that his sister was his mother and his mother was his grandmother. I know, mind trip, right? So I had to play it cool. I gave him my birth name and asked if he could check if that rang any bells with her.

He didn't reply for several days. I constantly refreshed the chat but thought I had scared him off. Then, one day, he wrote back and simply said, 'Well, it looks like you're my brother.'

We clicked very quickly and I was relieved to discover that we were undeniably similar. Though he still had a fairly close relationship with our mother, she had declined to comment when he had approached her about my existence. Of course it would have been lovely to have an open channel of communication with her, not because I needed or wanted anything from her, but merely to get a sense of where I came from. But I had no intention of being a grenade in her life that could potentially blow up her marriage all these years later. It was enough for me to have found a sibling who I could relate to and chat with from time to time. It did make me feel a little guilty, however. Though he was also musically inclined and had wanted to develop that more, he hadn't had the same opportunities I'd had, and I could sense a bit of jealousy that my adoption had provided me with that. I also felt ashamed that I had resented certain parts of my own upbringing, as it sounded like I really was far better off despite the underlying issues I was facing.

Having said that, I do have to admit that I had also done a bit of a stalk through his Facebook profile and managed to find our mother's page through it. From what I could see of the life she presented online, she had a far more relaxed outlook on life than my own mother. Life could have been a lot easier without that level of judgemental control.

Out of respect for her, I didn't contact her, and still haven't to this day. But I did spend hours going through everything she had posted – all her pictures, likes and comments. One stuck out to me in particular. It was a photo of a dirty car window on which someone had scribbled the words 'Kyle is gay' in perfect finger-point cursive. Our mother had commented, 'Whatever you choose to be.' To me, this showed an acceptance that meant, had I remained her son, that perhaps the deep psychological issues around my sexuality caused by my adoptive parents and their lifestyle might not have been part of my life. Maybe I would have received the freedom and encouragement I had needed during development that could have potentially prevented the self-esteem issues my parents' Catholicism had caused. What if my brother and I had switched places? As a heterosexual male, he could have thrived in their environment, while I would have grown up with confidence in who I was at my core. But that was not the way the cookie had crumbled. It seemed that both my half-brother and I had equal reason to think that the grass was greener on the other's side.

One of the fundamental principles taught to us in my Opus Dei school was that there must be full knowledge of a sinful act in order for a person to be punished for it. Therefore, had I never grown up with the idea that my homosexuality was a sin, I would never have experienced the mental trauma that my religious upbringing had caused. And even *if* it had turned out to be the grave sin they purported it to be, I wouldn't suffer the ravages of hell due to my lack of knowledge. It was therefore only by the blessing of my adoption that I was cursed with that knowledge. Biologically, my nature dictated that I would have been gay either way.

On the flip side, however, I couldn't deny the opportunities I had received by way of my adoption, and how they had led to the fulfilment in my career. And aside from the gay stuff, I value so many of the moral lessons I learned from the life I did live.

There are so many things that I am grateful for in the way my parents raised me. There is something beautiful and wholesome within the Catholic Church's teachings. To me, it all boils down to being good to one another. Being generous, accepting, caring and loving toward the people in our lives, and striving to be a good person in everything we do. It teaches us discipline and the value of moderation in our lives. It teaches humility and kindness. And it provides a sense of hope. Though the delivery of some values were at odds with the message itself, these were the core lessons I had gleaned from them.

This was how I had been nurtured, and I do strive each day to be a good person and make a positive impact in people's lives. I am also grateful to have been taught the value of hard work and the necessity of patience, as these lessons have helped me through times of real struggle. I am proud to have these qualities, and it is thanks to my parents, my mum in particular. She was generous to a fault, and always had time for everyone. Though she was misguided in many ways, her discipline in her faith was admirable and she was a light in so many people's lives. I hope to one day be able to pay forward those traits through my own children. I would be so proud to see even just a glimpse of their grandmother reflected in their eyes.

***

As I sat on the plane back to Los Angeles on my way to move in with Liam, a person I barely knew, these were the thoughts swirling in my head. I wasn't concentrating on the irrational decision I was making at that moment. My mind was occupied by something far more existential. I was contemplating my very nature. My nature was what I had been born with and, ultimately, had nothing to do with the parents who had raised me. It was my nature that had given me my musical abilities and my thirst to be a performer. Nature had given me my personality, sensitivity and sense of humour. Heck, nature had dictated my hairline, eye colour and even my gustatory orientation – which foods my tastebuds were partial to, and which they weren't interested in. And it was nature that had determined my sexuality.

Nature *is* what we are born with, and if God is our creator and was the one who deemed it so, then who are others to question and judge the nature of another person – which, by extension, means questioning and judging God himself?

Or perhaps I was just telling myself this to feel better about what I was about to do. A feeling in the pit of my stomach instinctually alerted me to the fact that something was wrong about this scenario, but it was too difficult to decipher. The red flags of this new relationship, with such an unknown person, were clouded in a haze of these existential concerns. I was uneasy that my responsible life plan had now disintegrated because of the events of the last few days, and I was improvising. I worried about my financial stability. I was saddened by the falling-out with my sister and felt quite alone in the world. My family had changed so much, and I didn't belong. I was terrified of the sin I was committing, and begged God to understand my decision and forgive me. The fate of my eternal soul hung in the balance, and I knew that I was condemning it to the fiery pits of hell. This was all completely unknown territory, and I didn't know who I was anymore.

It was a freefall, and I was clutching at any hanging vine I could to try and gain even the smallest semblance of stability. I prayed that I would be okay. I even prayed to Mum and asked her, if she was indeed out there, to look out for me. I had faith in myself and the career that I had been building, and felt that all I needed was time, position and opportunity. Los Angeles seemed to promise that, and at least I had someone in my life who loved me and wanted me around. I had misgivings about absolutely everything, but thought I was being brave by forging ahead. But what I *was* doing, without realising it at the time, was putting all the pressure on the success of the relationship. I needed it to be the best decision I'd ever made in order to justify the drastic life choice I was making. This meant that when things got bad, and boy did they get bad, I got lost in denial.

As you may have guessed, the decision to move in with Liam *wasn't* the best decision I ever made. It was the worst.

CHAPTER ELEVEN

Rose-Coloured Glasses

After my sleepless fourteen-hour life crisis at 10,000 metres, I walked out of LAX, breathed in the polluted air and had to accept that I had no choice but to stick with my decision to choose Liam over the family that had consistently let me down. And as I tried to suppress my misgivings, there he was – like something out of a high fashion catalogue, with his perfect hair and perfect clothes, leaning against his fancy sports car that glistened in the morning sun. My heart skipped a beat, and the painful whirlwind of the past few days was replaced by a feeling that I was living out my romance-movie fantasy.

For the first time in my twenty-eight years, I was experiencing that all-encompassing, on-cloud-nine, lose-my-mind kind of love – filled with butterflies, romantic notes and messages, as well as the exuberant flamboyance of being wrapped up entirely in another person, but also the rose-coloured glasses that blind you to the red flags that are right before your eyes.

The car sailed under the iconic LA palm trees lining Sunset Boulevard. We stopped for lunch at the world-famous Grove.

We drove through the historic Hollywood Hills, and I couldn't help but be swept away by the romance of it all. However, when we arrived at Liam's place, which I would now be calling home, something didn't match up with the way he had so far presented himself. His apartment was in a sketchy area of North Hollywood. It was down a small alleyway – the kind with minimal lighting, crumbling apartment buildings with unkempt grass, rusted stripped-out cars on front lawns and homeless tents occupying the sidewalk. Aside from not feeling very safe there, it just seemed at odds with the image he had so far curated.

Our complex, however, did have a security gate, which was a little peace of mind, but it was an old rundown building. It had two levels that wrapped around a paved courtyard with a dead palm tree wilting in the centre. A few of the yellow hallway lights were out, and the rest were blinking, giving it that 'It's your last night alive' feel, and the apartment itself was tiny. But what took me by surprise most of all was that the majority of the furniture in his apartment was *mine*. Apart from what I had given him, there was very little else in there. All he owned was a couch and a mirror, it seemed. He had my bedside drawers, TV and cabinet in the bedroom, with the only other piece of furniture being his bed, which was just a mattress on the floor. The microwave, coffee machine, pots, pans, cutlery and plates in the kitchen were also mine. So had he owned basically nothing when I had met him? And yet he was driving around in an expensive car and had a seemingly endless supply of seasonably fashionable outfits?

I immediately felt a touch uneasy. But instead of paying attention to that feeling, I swept my concerns under the rug because I was so completely swept up by him – by his charm, his charisma, his beauty and the fact that, unlike my family, he genuinely wanted to be around me. I had committed to this decision and I had to make it work.

I made a budget spreadsheet for us to follow, splitting the monthly costs of living. With my visa expenses growing, and now not being able to work while going through that process, I was living off savings and needed to make my money stretch. Liam apparently had some money coming in 'soon' from a modelling job he had done but, when our first joint rent and utilities bills came, he asked me to take care of it all. The same went for his car repayment and insurance. That cheque he was waiting on seemed permanently stuck in limbo. When another month rolled around, he made the same request. And when it came to Christmas time, I paid for all the gifts he gave to his parents, sister, nephews and grandmother – all of whom I had yet to meet.

That fateful night when I met Liam had been his birthday. His thirty-fourth birthday. It was only now that I was living with him that I realised that Liam was a 34-year-old American man with no job, no prospects, no real career achievements, no work ethic, no drive and, most importantly, no money. But he had entitlement in spades. He believed that normal jobs were beneath him – he was *far too beautiful and talented for that.* And yet I never saw him attend any model castings or auditions. I never saw him writing new songs or sending out his demo tracks. He genuinely believed that success would find *him*. Whenever I pointed out to him that the hustle would never end and we had to constantly put ourselves out there like I was doing, he would tell me that he believed in the power of manifestation and that he was *manifesting* his success. I urged him, at least, to reach out to the job that owed him money and make sure he got paid. Well, it turned out that he hadn't exactly been honest about that. It was, in fact, for a commercial from a few years earlier that he was an extra in. An extra. One of the other models from that shoot, who he remained friends with, had recently received a hefty royalty cheque for it, as she had been heavily featured in it. Liam just had a feeling that he deserved one, too, and had based all of his promises on that feeling.

We had been living together for a few months by this point, and I had been paying for everything – every meal, every coffee, every pack of his cigarettes, every bottle of vodka, every expensive psychiatrist appointment so he could get his prescription of Adderall and, obviously, the Adderall itself. Not to mention rent, utilities and his car. As the months went on, the amount that he was constantly promising to repay me was well into the thousands and climbing. My savings were haemorrhaging and, with my visa application soon to be filed, I had many big expenses to take care of there, too.

It was stressful. To say that I was upset that he had put all of his financial hopes in a cheque that never existed would be putting it mildly. As if to prove to me that he deserved to be paid for it, he showed me the commercial. He pointed to himself and the model who received the royalty. She was essentially the main character of the commercial, while over her shoulder, way in the background, the unrecognisable blurry dot surrounded by other blurry dots was Liam. My rose-coloured glasses started to slip, and I began to see him as someone who was either deluded, dishonest or both. He also seemed blissfully unconcerned with the amount of pressure he was placing on me, and rarely showed any gratitude for me taking care of his every need.

I did feel kind of sorry for him, though. He had so much potential and, for a brief moment, several years earlier, it had looked like maybe things were going in the right direction for him. But by the time we had met, he was in complete denial that he wasn't succeeding in a cutthroat world that required constant focus and drive. Perhaps he felt that getting a normal job would mean admitting defeat. I understood that, but life costs money and I had to put my foot down and insist that he find a way to bring some money into our relationship. Still, instead of making an effort to find employment, he just called his parents and started to get regular handouts from them, though I never really saw much proof of existence of that money. It was coincidentally around this time that he stopped asking me for money for cigarettes, booze and his Adderall, though his consumption of them never dwindled.

Soon, I had no choice but to start paying the rent using my credit card. Everything about the carefully laid plan I had made a year before had fallen by the wayside. I had blown my budget by more than double, with no money coming in and no sight of the thousands of dollars he owed me. Finally, however, my visa was approved and, though restrictive in the kinds of work I was allowed to do, I managed to get a job working for Abercrombie & Fitch at Universal Studios. But on less than ten dollars an hour, it became very difficult to make ends meet.

Liam's refusal to work led to some lengthy arguments between us, and the moment they got too real, he would go out for a smoke and often returned with a fresh bottle of vodka. Then, one day, I turned up for a shift at A&F and he was there. Without telling me, he had successfully interviewed for a management position at the place he *knew* I was working at. So now he was my boss, too. While it might seem that this level of pettiness is unbelievable, I do think that he was jealous that I had become an Abercrombie boy – modelling was *his* thing and his fragile ego needed to know that he was beautiful enough to get a job there as well.

I was starting to feel really stuck at this point. I thought I was in love with Liam. He had filled the void left by my family's rejection, and I had taken such a huge risk by committing to this relationship. I needed a sense of belonging somewhere. But, having said that, by now he had bled me dry. I started to see a therapist, when I could afford a session. She introduced me to the idea of co-dependency, which was a concept that I didn't comprehend. Essentially, it meant we were tied together due to our need for each other. But that sounded a lot like my relationship with my mother, so I was confused. However, the way he needed me was not so much as a boyfriend but more as a wallet. I began to notice that I was somehow becoming quite forgetful of my credit card, continually misplacing it. It would turn up on the kitchen counter, coffee table or TV cabinet, even though I always kept it in my wallet. How strange.

One morning, I woke up and Liam and the car were gone. He didn't have a shift at work and hadn't told me he had anything on that morning. I tried to reach him without success. I walked down the road to do a grocery shop, only to discover that my credit card had mysteriously vanished from my wallet yet again. It was intensely awkward leaving a full shopping cart at the check-out and I was too embarrassed to show my face there for months. When Liam eventually arrived home, he had a couple of Starbucks coffees and bagels in his hands. He was also carrying a brand-new outfit from Zara. He told me he had been sent on a model casting last minute, but, when he got there, the casting director didn't like his outfit and had given him $100 to buy himself something better. You know, because casting directors tend to give out their money like that.

All I asked was where my credit card was. He suggested I look under the mattress. I had turned the place upside down after I got back from the grocery store and had looked under every surface multiple times, including the mattress. Yet sure enough, after he suggested I look again, there it magically was.

I logged onto my account and saw a couple of charges from that morning. One to the tune of $100 at – you guessed it – Zara, and the other for Starbucks. I started to scroll through the past several months of my account, picking up on more and more suspicious transactions and withdrawals that I knew I hadn't made. It was a similar feeling to the day I discovered my father's infidelity. I was finding out something that I didn't want to believe was true, so I kept looking for reasons not to believe what I was seeing. And yet all I saw was more evidence.

A few transactions stood out to me. They were from several weeks prior, when he had supposedly spent the weekend visiting his family in San Diego. He had asked to borrow my card for the weekend so he could get petrol for the car. I had stupidly agreed and taken out cash to get me through the few days he would be gone. And yet, on my bank statements, there were charges to a swanky hotel bar in Hollywood over that weekend. A place I had never visited in my life. Rather than bringing up the entire issue, I asked him only about those particular charges. It turned out he had never gone to San Diego. He had spent that weekend just down the road in the Hollywood Hills, with his ex.

Though we had spent months together by now, believe it or not, we still had not slept together. I know it sounds confusing, but even though I had lost my virginity already, I had regretted that. I had gone to confession about it, and I guess a part of me thought – or at the very least hoped – that God would recognise that, while I was living with my boyfriend, I was still trying to remain as pure as possible. Liam had never once pressured me for sex. He seemed quite content with the way things were, and I had honestly appreciated that and viewed it as support. However, when confronted with the charges on my credit card, he argued that if I had been *putting out* for him, he wouldn't have had to cheat. Those charges, therefore, were *my fault*.

I went for a long walk to clear my head. I couldn't believe that, on top of owing me so much money at this point and relying on my generosity, he had been stealing from me *and* cheating on me. I had been stressed out of my mind and miserable for months now but had been too embarrassed to admit to my friends that things hadn't been going well. To them, I had painted a picture that I was blissfully happy. They were all so pleased that I was finally *out and proud,* and it was too humiliating to admit that things weren't working out. I was close to broke, thanks to Liam, and wouldn't have been able to afford a different living situation at the time, so I felt I had no choice but to stick it out. And, despite everything, I also loved him. I felt sorry for him and wanted to help. I wanted him to reach the potential that I saw he had. And it broke my heart to think of him without me, because I knew how much he needed me. I had come out to my family because of him. I had made a huge life decision because of him. I needed it to work out. So the stupid conclusion I came to, by the end of my walk, was that it was time to finally sleep with him. Sex would secure him to me.

There are two kinds of virginities that a gay boy can lose. There's the easy one, and there's the hard one. You are either the plug or the socket. The evening I spent with my celebrity crush, I was the plug. On this occasion, I was the socket. Though, in hindsight, he wasn't a boy with a huge amount of heft down there, it was still my first time and it wasn't a pleasant experience. I immediately started to bleed afterward and I cried for half an hour in the shower, panicking that the blood wasn't stopping. It was absolutely the worst decision to have made in that moment and I knew it. I felt weak, stupid, humiliated and trapped. If only I had a family I could call for help, but that wasn't an option. It was just another thing I had to keep to myself while still putting on a brave face for everyone around.

While all this was going on, I had still been auditioning regularly, and getting tantalisingly close to some incredible roles in big TV and film projects. I knew I was in a toxic relationship and was miserable, looking for a way out. But I just needed to keep surviving until I eventually landed one of those roles so that I could finally be free. And I knew a thing or two about survival. I had built up a callus over the years to the feeling of being miserable in your own home, yearning for release. And just like I did when I was a teenager, I put all my focus and energy into my career dreams and fantasised about that inevitable day when all this would be far behind me. I knew I could do it. I just needed to shut off a little. To everyone else, however, I kept up the pretence that everything was fine.

One of my friends, Russ, who was my best mate Dave's roommate in LA, had also started working at Abercrombie & Fitch. I know he noticed the tension between me and

Liam, and to his credit he did give me many opportunities to open up about what was really going on, but I never took the chance. It was far too humiliating to admit the truth.

Liam's behaviour began to get more and more erratic. He spoke to me almost constantly in a high-pitched, squeaky voice. It was a 'cartoon character' he had created in his mind. Her name was Juicy, and he would call me Jazmine. I got so used to it that it was odd to hear his regular speaking voice, which would mostly now be at work. He started to seek out every single karaoke night in town and drag me along because he lived for the compliments he received after he sang. Though I'd enjoyed karaoke as a fun novelty, I didn't like it enough to go every night of the week.

It started to seem a bit pathetic that he constantly needed to seek approval from drunken patrons in sleazy bars. We would even drive halfway to San Diego each week because a bar there held a weekly open-mic night where Liam knew he'd have a receptive audience of perhaps ten at most, including ourselves. But the bar manager liked him and would fix him up with free alcohol all night. I'd then have the pleasant task of driving the two hours home, with a drunk and Adderall-high Liam talking nonstop about how amazing his set had been, and repeating, word for word, all the compliments he had received.

This would have been tolerable if the open-mic night represented any actual opportunity for his music career. I wouldn't have minded so much if this bar was a known hotspot for record producers and music-label headhunters. But it wasn't. It was a small suburban bar in Temecula, located in a shopping mall car park, that seemed to mostly cater for the sixty-and-over crowd.

One night, he woke me up at 2 am, having had the sudden urge to drive to a Hollywood Hills lookout, stare up at the sky and do some 'manifesting'. It was cold, uncomfortable and exhausting, and he stopped on the way so that I could buy him some booze for the stargazing.

I was growing more and more concerned by his behaviour and wished that I could speak to one of his friends, as I started to feel that he was not well. But he didn't seem to have many long-term friends and he barely made an effort to see the ones he did have. He was far more concerned with making new friends and, each time he did, I would hear him regaling them with the same stories. He had a schtick and he was very good at winning people over with it. Just like I had, they would fall captive to his charm and charisma, and I was constantly being reminded by these people how lucky I was to have landed this amazing catch. However, almost like clockwork, when the novelty had worn off after a few weeks, he would dump these newfound besties and move on to find someone new to stroke his ego.

Not long after this, he invited two of our co-workers from Abercrombie & Fitch to come and live with us in our minuscule apartment. They were eighteen-year-old twins from Northern California who, like so many of us, had moved to Los Angeles in pursuit of the Hollywood dream. However, since arriving in town, they had been living in their car. Now the boys, thanks to my benevolent boyfriend, would be staying in our living room. They, too, provided an ego boost for Liam. They were naive, good-looking teenagers and they looked up to him as a mid-thirties success story. He was almost twice their age, but they lapped up his bullshit and revered him, as they were hearing all the grandiose tales of his supposed modelling and singing career for the first time. He would crack out the guitar and sit in the living room and sing to them for hours. The three of them would then prance around the car park and take photos of each other (but mostly just of him). Liam would sit for hours in the living room going through each photo, gushing frenetically about how incredibly good he looked.

'Oh my God, you guys, you know what we should do?' I heard him say to the twins one night. 'We should do the Charlie's Angels pose! Oh my GOD! We totally should!' He let out a shrill squeal of glee, and I heard furniture being moved around. I had been relaxing on the bedroom floor mattress but got up to see what was happening.

'Okay, I go in the middle. Do the finger gun!'

I walked in to see them posing in front of a propped-up camera phone.

'Oh my God, YES! HOT!' shouted Liam.

He was almost thirty-five by now, and yet as I looked at him in that moment, I felt like I was in a relationship with Ja'mie from *Summer Heights High*.

I was living in some sort of madhouse circus fever dream, and my boyfriend was behaving like a child. But I had made my choices.

There was no escaping Liam, because I would also see him at work. Though I was glad he was finally working, he never made any attempts at paying me back. He always talked about how he would *one day*, but I only ever saw him spend money on himself.

Through the twins, he found an endless supply of impressionable young people who would be responsive to his schtick. The boys were very attractive and seemed to meet other cute teenagers easily. Liam had a receptive new audience almost every night of the week, and we would go to the karaoke bars with them for the sole purpose of Liam putting on a show for his captive audience of teenagers. He was exhausting.

I was reaching the end of my tether when something truly deranged happened. One night, Liam texted me saying some friends of his were coming over to our place to hang out. He asked me to buy some vodka and frozen pizza so we could entertain them. He gave no further details. Like the dutiful lackey I was, I did what he asked, unsure of how we were meant to fit the four of us, and now this unconfirmed number of unknown people, in our tiny apartment to hang out. When he got home, he told me and the boys that the people coming over were none other than recent Academy Award winner Jennifer Lawrence, star of *The Hunger Games* and *Silver Linings Playbook*, and pop sensation Selena Gomez.

Why on earth would these Hollywood icons be taking a break from their glamorous and busy schedules to come and hang out in our tiny, run-down, crack-alley apartment complex?

I could see disbelief on the boys' faces too, but I simply didn't have it in me to make an issue out of it. I've always been a non-confrontational person, but I had also grown numb to his antics by then. I put the pizza in the oven and figured I'd just wait and see how the evening panned out. The four of us pre-gamed while the Hollywood glitterati partied somewhere in the Hills. We were the afterparty, apparently.

Suddenly, Liam's phone buzzed and he leaped up. 'They're here,' he said, instructing us to wait out of sight in the parking lot because he didn't want to scare off the celebs. He wanted to greet them by himself so that they could ease into things without us gawping fans rushing them and making them feel uncomfortable. He would come and get us when the moment was right.

Liam was gone for about ten minutes. It was well after midnight at this point and I was hungry and losing my patience. While we waited, one of the boys turned to me and asked, 'Yo, is this real?'

'I don't know, man.' I sighed with exasperation. 'Doubt it.'

Eventually Liam came back and I asked if we were allowed to finally eat the pizza. He said that Jennifer and Selena were in the car with their friends making plans. 'What plans?' I asked. 'Aren't *we* the plan?'

'Yeah,' he said, 'but, you know … they're actors.'

'So?' I asked. 'It took you this long to come and tell us?'

'Oh, well, Jennifer really needed to pee so I let her use the bathroom real quick,' he explained.

'Jennifer Lawrence just peed in our toilet?' I asked, not believing a word of it.

Thank God one of the boys spoke up at this point.

'Bullshit,' he said, shaking his head.

'Fine,' said Liam, bristling. 'Come on. I'll take you to them. You're probably going to scare them off, though.'

He started marching toward the front of the complex to take us out onto the street, where we would obviously see their slick SUV and say hi.

When we got to the street, to no-one's surprise, there was no car. Liam made a big show of running up and down the street to try and see where they'd gone, coming back feigning frustration. 'You can't trust these Hollywood types. They're all so flaky.'

'You're full of shit,' said one of the boys.

'You don't believe me?' snapped Liam. 'I'll prove it to you!'

He led us into the apartment and opened up the oven.

'I gave Jennifer a slice of pizza because she was hungry,' he said. And, sure enough, a piece was missing. *Sure*, I thought.

'And look!' he continued, 'She left some of her jewellery in the bathroom.'

He picked up a cheap bracelet on the bathroom sink and waved his smoking-gun evidence in our faces. Except the bracelet was something I had been given during the previous year's Emmys gifting suite – a tradition during awards season, when TV and film personalities are invited to swanky hotels and receive free goodie bags and products from various companies who only ask for a photo of the celeb holding the product in return.

It was a cheap stretch-lace bracelet with a large fake pearl dangling from the wrist.

'Pretty sure that's actually mine,' I said. 'From the gifting suite?'

'Obviously she went to the same gifting suite,' Liam replied condescendingly.

I looked at him in disbelief. The whole night had been completely deranged, and I was worn out. The boys were in shock. I had a slice of stone-cold pizza and went to bed without another word.

The next day, the boys opted to move back into their car. Apart from being weirded out by Liam, they could sense the storm that was about to erupt.

We fought all day and night, into the early hours of the morning. Everything that had been bottling up for months exploded. All the false promises, the owed money, the cheating, the thieving, the lies, the outrageous behaviour. I'm ashamed to admit this, but it did get physical on both sides. A neighbour was banging on the walls due to the noise. Liam put his hands on me, one hand over my mouth to shut me up and the other around my neck. And I defended myself. I landed a solid punch in the middle of his face, and then it was an all-out boxing match. I'm not proud of it.

At around 3 am, sporting multiple bruises, I called my best mate Dave. He and my other best mate Russ were roommates who lived not too far away. Though it was late, Dave immediately raced over and collected me. When he arrived, Liam cowered behind the couch as if it had been a one-sided attack.

'Look what he did to me,' he said to Dave. 'He's a maniac!'

'What?' I shouted.

Dave put his hand on my arm. 'Don't, mate. Let's just go.'

I quickly stuffed a suitcase and left.

As Russ had already noticed that something wasn't quite right between us, it was easier to finally be honest with him and Dave. I filled them in on everything that had transpired over the last several months. But as the adrenaline of the fight subsided and the reality of what had just happened sank in, I collapsed onto the couch and crumpled into a bawling mess. I couldn't control my emotions. I was hyperventilating, unable to catch my breath, while loud wails erupted from my chest. The pain of my first heartbreak hurt more than the physical injuries I had just sustained.

Russ and Dave were incredibly patient with me. They sat on either side of me and held me as I rocked back and forth, blood pouring from my nose. No-one had ever seen me like this before, and I could tell by their stunned looks that they were worried about me, and perhaps a little scared.

The first thing we needed to do was collect all my belongings from the apartment – my TV, my furniture, my piano keyboard, my iPad, my coffee machine, my PlayStation, my pots and pans, my remaining clothes. I also had a $3500 camera that I had bought as a gift for myself right before moving to LA so I could tape my auditions and practise photography.

We waited a day for things to cool down a bit. Then, flanked by my best mates, I returned to the apartment. It was empty except for his mattress and couch and a few small items that didn't belong to me. Everything else that I owned was gone. Stolen.

Liam wasn't answering his phone or my texts. And yet he knew I would be seeing him at work in just a couple of days. I was now in such a bad financial position that I had no choice but to continue working with him as my manager.

The day of my next shift, I received a text from him. He admitted that he had taken all of my possessions. He had sold them to various pawn shops all around Hollywood and the valley. He blamed me, of course.

'It's the first of the month,' he texted. 'You left me and I had to pay rent somehow!'

'That's called theft, Liam,' I wrote back. 'Borrow more money from your parents or something, but get my stuff back NOW!'

'They've cut me off,' he replied. 'I don't get what the big deal is, you'll get your stuff back as soon as I get paid.'

Though I didn't believe his words anymore, I felt I would still be able to hold him accountable. It was inconceivable to me that anyone, even him, could get away with something of this scale. *At least he had a job*, I thought, so I knew he wasn't lying about a pay cheque coming his way this time. And I would be seeing him almost every day, so I could keep tabs on him.

Having said that, I kept my distance from him at work, not wanting to cause a scene and risk losing my job. Meanwhile, he was acting like nothing had happened at all: laughing, joking around, being loud and flamboyant as usual. As our pay cheques came and went, I still hadn't received anything from him. And any time I would try to approach him to discuss it, he would find an excuse to scurry away.

I resorted to texting his mum. In response, she called me and, with a sigh that spoke a thousand words, she started to tell me stories from his past. Similar stories of well-positioned ex-boyfriends with enough money for a comfortable lifestyle, Liam never contributing, theft, erratic behaviour, physical abuse. She then let me in on a little secret. Liam had been married to a woman about ten years prior. They had met when they were both music leaders at a religious youth centre. Liam's father was in the construction business and had built them a house as a wedding present. Within a week of their wedding, his wife had caught him cheating on her with a man and moved out immediately. Liam, however, hadn't told anyone and remained living in the house for months, coming up with creative excuses as to why no-one ever saw his wife around. His mother apologised for the fact that I had been caught up in his drama and said she would do her best to ensure Liam did the right thing by me. But that never happened.

I contacted the police, but they were unable to help me. Not only did I not have receipts for anything, but even if I did, I'd need to know the exact pawnshop locations that my items had been taken to in order to claim them. I eventually made a humiliating call to my dad and confessed everything that happened.

'Well,' he said, 'I guess you just have to move on.'

I stayed with Dave and Russ for the rest of that month. Out of the kindness of their hearts, they didn't ask me for rent during that time. Dave was about to move back to Australia to get married, so I could take over his room once he left; I just had to make sure I could afford it.

I used that month to save up every penny I earned. I took more shifts, which meant seeing Liam more and more at work. And I spent next to nothing. I walked to and from work for forty-five minutes each way so as not to spend anything on travel. I froze my gym membership and ate next to nothing.

A few days before the new month, with rent on the horizon, I had just finished a long shift at A&F and was too exhausted and hungry to start the walk home just yet. I stopped outside of the food court at Universal Studios and decided to check my bank account to see if I had enough money to spoil myself with a five-dollar Subway six-inch for dinner – a rare treat those days. By my calculations, I had saved enough to pay my dues with just a smidge left over. But, just like the apartment had been, my bank account was empty.

This was simply not possible. I had spent absolutely nothing on myself. And yet, lo and behold, Liam's car payment and insurance had been withdrawn from my account that very day. He had copied down my card details and was still using me as his personal piggy bank. I slumped into my seat, exhausted, starving and with no idea what on earth I was going to do next. This was the lowest point in my life.

The universe, however, chose this exact moment to provide me with a lifeline. As I sat there, drawing stares from tourists who were seeing a 29-year-old man openly weeping in a theme park food court, my Australian talent agent called me. I had been offered a leading role in a film shooting back home in Australia. I hadn't auditioned for it and had no idea what it was. But it was a well-paid acting job, which covered flights and accommodation, and an escape from the nightmare I was living in. Of course I accepted the role. My agent was somewhat bewildered, asking if I might want to read the script first. But no, I didn't care what it was. I accepted the role and, two days later, I was on a flight to Queensland to shoot my new film titled *Red Billabong.*

I read the script on the plane. It wasn't great, but it wasn't awful. It was a uniquely Australian take on a creature feature and had some cool action sequences and stunts. The role was also a very different character for me, and I was excited by the opportunity to try something different. And it wasn't lost on me that it was something of a miracle that this fell into my lap exactly when I needed it.

A few weeks into the production of the film, however, the cast and crew started to notice that no-one was getting paid. One morning I received a call from my agent telling me to not go to set that day. A stop-work meeting had been called and the crew had walked off. As happens from time to time in the film industry, the financial guarantees set in place at the commencement of a production had fallen through. I had no doubt that the producers were working tirelessly to fix their issues, but as it stood, there was simply no way to continue with the production for the time being. As this was, technically, a breach of contract, the production company had to pay me out my full fee while they figured out their next moves. They had also already paid for my accommodation in full for the entire two-month shoot of the film. I could either stay in my free accommodation on the gorgeous golden sands of Queensland or return to LA. I decided to stick to Queensland. I had a huge amount of money coming my way, and a free ride for another month, and let's face it, I needed a fucking break.

Initially, I used the time to sleep in, get back into a healthy diet and exercise schedule, and decompress from the tumultuous time that I had had. But, without the work to distract me, I was left with a broken heart. It had obviously been a toxic and abusive relationship – which I can say now, with ten years of distance – but it was my first heartbreak and I was as naive and immature as a teenager being dumped by their high school crush. My mind started playing tricks on me and all I could think about were the good times and the excitement I had felt when I first met Liam. I needed someone to talk some sense into me. When I tried to talk about the break-up with my sister, she sent me a link to a support group for Catholic gay men who were learning how to be straight. There were seminars, workshops, camps and an online forum for the men to discuss their sexuality problem.

It was disappointing. Rather than empathising with my situation, she was taking another opportunity to try and change me without engaging with the real issues at play. I had a phone call with her where I expressed the heartbreak I was feeling, and she replied, 'Tim, you know what I think about this.' She did, however, invite me to her daughter's birthday dinner, so I flew down to Sydney and drove to her place with a cousin. After the cake had been consumed and the kids had gone to bed, my sister's husband awkwardly excused himself from the room. My sister and cousin then turned to me in unison, and the temperature in the room seemed to rise. It was an ambush. The birthday party had been a trick. The reason I was there was really an intervention. They lectured me about being gay, told me over and over to 'give it up', and urged me to consider the conversion camp or, at the very least, seek counsel from a Catholic priest. It reminded me of when Mum had tricked me into seeing the psychologist for hypnotherapy. I told them I didn't appreciate the lecture and said I would make my own way home. My sister lived pretty remotely so it was a long walk, but I was disgusted by their actions and had no other options. After about half an hour walking down the highway, my cousin pulled up in her car.

'Get in the car,' she yelled. 'You're being stupid.'

I ignored her.

'It will take you hours to get back,' she insisted.

'I don't care!' I shouted back. 'I'm done with you people fucking me over!'

Cars on the highway started to honk at her as her vehicle crawled along beside me. Eventually, thanks to some common sense, I relented. This cousin and I had always been quite close. She had lived with my family for a few years and, after Mum died, had kept me company more than most. It was really hurtful that, like my sister, she had ganged up on me in this way. As she drove she tried to talk with me, but I didn't respond. It was a quiet forty-minute journey back to where I was staying. When we got there, I slammed the door shut and we have never seen or spoken to each other since.

I had literally only flown to Sydney to attend my niece's birthday, which, it turned out, had been a mistake. After the events of that dramatic evening, I flew back to Queensland and was once again left alone with my thoughts. My mental health was at an all-time low. On top of mourning my relationship, I was now dealing with what had just happened with my sister and cousin. I had bent over backward for my family, and this was the thanks that I got. I started to feel a pit, not in my stomach, but in the very essence of who I was. My as-yet-undiagnosed adoption abandonment issues started to hit me hard. Every love that I had ever had in my life was now gone. I felt empty and unlovable. I sank into a deep depression.

And then all of a sudden, while I was in this incredibly fragile state, Liam started to get in touch with me again, love-bombing me with 'I miss you's and 'I love you's. I didn't think of myself as a weak person but, given how vulnerable I was at the time, I succumbed to the attention he was giving me. Soon, we were in touch every day. Love bomb after love bomb – just like it had been at the beginning, and I fell for it all over again.

As I've come to learn about abusive relationships, a strong tie holds the two toxic people together. It has been shown time and time again that the abused person tends to go back to their abuser. For me, this was due to a fundamental lack of self-esteem and self-worth. I didn't know myself well enough to make healthy, self-respectful choices. I didn't love myself enough to stand up for myself. I had never experienced what respect in love looks like. And with the giant gaping hole in my heart left by my family, my judgement was clouded.

By then, the film had paid me out the remainder of my contracted fee and, for the first time since meeting Liam, I was back to being comfortably saved up. A silly little voice in my head suggested that things had blown out of proportion between us due to the financial strain we had been under, and now that issue had been resolved, maybe things would be different. Maybe he had learned and grown from the experience, too. The potential that I had always seen in him was just under the surface, ready to be extracted. Maybe, just maybe, I could fix him …

I listened to that silly little voice and decided that I needed to make some sort of grand romantic gesture to reboot our relationship and rekindle our love. Something like giving him an all-expenses-paid round trip to spend time with me in Australia and New Zealand for ten days. So that's what I did.

Liam still hadn't returned my belongings. He hadn't paid me back a cent for the months of his shirked financial responsibilities and theft over the time we had lived together, and he hadn't uttered a single word of apology for any of it. But my denial was strong. Naive, deluded, damaged and unloved little me thought that maybe this holiday would win him back to me and prove my worth to him. And maybe that would encourage him to try harder this time.

I spent a completely irrational and irresponsible amount of money on hotels and experiences in Queenstown, New Zealand, to make it a perfect romantic getaway. Within an hour of picking him up from the airport, however, I regretted everything about my decision. Almost the first words out of his mouth were a complaint that I hadn't given him business class tickets because he had been so uncomfortable on the flight in economy. He also didn't want to do much sightseeing due to jet lag and, by the time we arrived in New Zealand, I had already decided that this was a completely futile enterprise. But, as the money had already been spent, I figured I'd soak up as much of the experience as I could, and not allow this raincloud of a human to take away from the crisp mountain air, the crystal-clear turquoise waters and grand majesty of the staggering alps. I loved New Zealand and I was determined to enjoy myself.

We both returned to Los Angeles at the end of the trip. I made it clear I wouldn't be moving back in with him and still expected my stuff back. Our communication dwindled after that, but he still stayed in touch – hitting me with sweet texts and making a point to remind me of the happier times. And on my side, though I hate to admit it, a very small ember of feeling remained. But I was learning, and I did my best to not fall for his old tricks.

A few weeks after getting back to LA, I was approached at the gym by an incredibly handsome man named Scott. I was flabbergasted when he approached me and asked me out. Not one part of me thought that a guy like him would ever notice me. But I figured that the best way to purge Liam from my system, once and for all, was to try and move on. So I accepted.

The evening of our date, Liam got in touch and said he wanted to see me that night. It was almost as if he was psychic (which he claimed to be, by the way). Why couldn't he just leave me alone? I tried to shut him down and told him I had the flu and was staying home for the night.

Scott was distractingly handsome, put together and interesting. We had a lovely night out and went back to his place after. It was very wholesome. I told him I wouldn't be sleeping with him and he was very respectful of that. But I won't deny that there was a significant amount of kissing involved.

Suddenly, I felt my phone vibrating in my pocket. There were dozens of missed calls and texts from Liam. I felt a sinking feeling. Then my roommate Russ sent me a text.

Um, dude? Liam is here. He just jumped the fence of the apartment complex and was banging at the door. Did you tell him you were sick? He barged past me and checked every room looking for you. Now he's freaking out in the living room.

I told Scott I needed to get home. I made up some story about being too tempted to go too far with him and, as a perfect gentleman, he accepted this and drove me home. I gave him a quick kiss as I got out of his car.

Unfortunately, Liam still hadn't left. He was sitting in his car across the street and had seen that interaction. I was caught out ... for doing something I had every right in the world to do. Yes, I had lied to him. But he wasn't my partner anymore and I owed him absolutely nothing.

That, I am glad to tell you, was the final exclamation point in the saga. Liam had been given a million second chances. The outrage he exhibited about me daring to live my own life and attempt to move on was, finally, proof that he was toxic beyond measure, and completely irredeemable. If anyone had a right to that level of outrage, it was me. In total, he owed me somewhere in the vicinity of US$25,000 at least, including all of my belongings that he had sold for chump change to fuel his alcohol and Adderall addiction.

Of course I never got anything back from him.

I did, however, have a few small wins. Years after we had stopped speaking, I found out that he had started using my credit card to make his car payments again, for not an insignificant amount. The absolute nerve of it. I was able to put a stop to those payments and get reimbursed by the insurance company as I was able to prove that the payments were for a car and policy that weren't in my name. It wasn't long before some mutual friends of ours told me that he was playing the victim card yet again, begging for handouts from them with some tall tale about someone stealing $2000 from him. He also lost his job at Abercrombie & Fitch because he had been caught stealing clothes.

A couple of his other exes who had similar stories of being used, stolen from and taken advantage of reached out to me. One of them was a 21-year-old kid who had moved from North Carolina to pursue a modelling career in Hollywood with little more than the clothes on his back. Once Liam had dried him out, he too had been cast aside. This poor young man had heard horror stories about me, but after his own experience with Liam, he had contacted me hoping to get some sort of clarity and closure. Liam would have been about thirty-seven at the time. I was appalled that he would pick on someone so young and vulnerable. And yet I saw many similarities between myself and this kid. We were both out-of-towners with big dreams and families who didn't support our career choices or sexuality, making us both very naive and vulnerable to his practised veneer of charm and charisma, all designed so he could maintain a life for himself that required as little effort as possible. A parasite, basically. And lastly, a few years later, I ran into a fellow gay actor-friend of mine who told me he and Liam had had a one-night stand, and when he woke up the next morning, not only was Liam gone, but so was the $500 in cash he'd had in his wallet.

The thing about being conned, or being in an abusive relationship with someone like this, is that you feel so incredibly stupid about the decisions you made during that time. I was so embarrassed that I had fallen for it and that I had allowed the behaviour to continue for so long. It was humiliating. I had thought that I was mature, and that I had enough nous to not be so easily fooled and taken advantage of.

There were of course other people he'd used and conned, too. I came to realise that we had all been ripe for the picking for a guy like him, as our upbringing, lack of experience and lack of support had left us all with low self-worth and little to no self-esteem. With families who had required us to constantly pretend and people-please in order to survive, we had all internalised the belief that love and pain went hand in hand. We were used to constantly ignoring our own wants and needs in order to make the people we loved happy. In my case, I had also been taught that it was a religious virtue.

I wished I had been more confident in myself. But I was really only just starting to discover who I actually was. At least, through this entire ordeal, I had finally realised that coming out wasn't as easy as a snap of the fingers – it was just the beginning of my self-education. I was now tasked with relearning everything and drawing my own conclusions about what *I* believed, what morals *I* held dear and how *I* wanted to be for the rest of my life.

CHAPTER TWELVE

Take Two

Unfortunately, there wasn't a handbook to help guide me through the process of finding myself. It's one of those things that was meant to happen during childhood and adolescence, with the safety net of family support to cushion the blow when mistakes inevitably happened. Because I had long-held beliefs that worked against my very nature, it was incredibly difficult to shed the constant inner monologue of, *This is wrong. I shouldn't be doing this. I am going to hell.* How could I possibly differentiate between what felt scary because of the beliefs that had been drilled into me, and what felt scary simply because it was new and I had absolutely no idea what I was doing?

It took me several years on my journey of self-discovery to find the ability to relax into my identity as a gay person. It was only when I really did relax into it that I could truly be myself and become available to the right people, whether they be friends or partners. In fact, it was somewhere around mid-2018, five years after coming out, that I finally stopped being offended if people assumed that I was gay. But much like the situation with Liam, it took many blunders and missteps to reach that point, along with some incredibly painful moments and difficult family conversations that were long overdue.

The process of finding myself was hindered by the fact that I was still paying the price for my relationship with Liam. The trip to New Zealand had been a bad error in judgement, not just because it was outrageous to let him back into my life after what he had put me through, but also because the cost of the trip was extravagant and incredibly irresponsible of me. I had been living off credit cards for a few months while with Liam, and now they were all chasing me for my debts. Even though *Red Billabong* had paid well, most of that money vanished to the credit card companies and I had another costly visa renewal on the horizon. I was also going through a dry spell as an actor. I completed *Red Billabong* in 2015, about a year after we initially started filming, and I shot another film at the end of that year, but LA was a difficult place to make ends meet, and the money coming in was not enough.

I ended up taking on four jobs at once, seven days a week. I'd be up at 5 am to open a pie shop in downtown Los Angeles. It was just off Skid Row, at the back of a dingy alley. It didn't feel safe, I was getting $10 an hour paid under the table, there were virtually no customers, and ghosts don't tip. I'd drive to the gym after my shift, and then have a quick lunch break at home before heading to my next job, hosting for a swanky rooftop bar in Hollywood with a clientele of famous models, musicians, actors and social media influencers. The pay was better there, but there weren't enough shifts to rely on. I'd finish work around midnight, often later, and would drive home as fast as I could to get as much sleep as possible, and do it all over again the next day. Most days I operated on four hours of sleep.

On days when I didn't work at the bar, I was paid to letter-drop junk mail and put posters on telegraph poles. On weekends, I worked at a sports nutrition store run by a man with a striking resemblance to Arnold Schwarzenegger. It also paid $10 an hour, and though there were commissions to be had, they had even fewer customers than the pie shop.

I had little to no time to prepare for auditions when they would come up, which took a toll on my performances. And so the cycle would continue.

Still looming large were the thoughts that it had all gone wrong because God was punishing me for giving in to my sexuality. My career had been doing pretty well while I was a closeted virgin, and everything seemed to fall apart the moment I dared to live as myself. These thoughts weren't just daily but hourly occurrences, and I had to focus on convincing myself that those thoughts had been planted there by people who knew no better and didn't understand the damage they had caused. I still attended mass on a weekly basis and still prayed deeply to God. By this time, I was no longer asking not to be gay anymore, because I knew that would never change. Instead, I prayed that God would accept me as a gay man and asked for the strength and bravery to forge ahead. It felt like stumbling through a maze blindfolded.

Meanwhile, unintentionally, not even six months after ending things with Liam, I found myself in a new relationship, with not nearly enough time in between to do the work on myself that I so desperately needed. Within a year, we would be engaged.

***

Ken and I met through a dating app. Well, that's generous. It was Grindr. I don't recommend finding a life partner on Grindr. Out of all the conversations I had had on there, however, he stood out in the maturity of the questions he was asking, and how genuinely interested he was in my life and getting to know me. I found him to be equally intriguing and enjoyed his quick wit and banter. I had used Grindr mostly to window-shop. I was still too scared to really enact its purpose, which is for casual sexual flings. So it was refreshing to have a conversation on there that made me feel like an actual person rather than an object to be used.

Ironically, I had been chatting with him before going to Sunday mass. When the mass ended, I eagerly pulled out my phone to continue the conversation and, in a burst of impulsivity, I asked him if we could go out for dinner. It was the first time I had actually wanted to go on a date since the failed attempt with Scotty, the gym hottie. Despite my previous relationship, I had never been on an actual date before I met Scott. So Ken was just my second. I was twenty-nine and woefully inexperienced.

I spent the months in between trying to return to an undramatic life. I also really wanted to destigmatise sex for myself, though that was easier said than done. I was very lucky to have met a lot of nice and respectful men along the way who hadn't made me feel uncomfortable, though I rarely met the expectations they had. Sex was far too scary for me. However, I had also met a few men who weren't so courteous. These encounters taught me some valuable lessons about boundaries and how to stick up for myself. I was determined to never have a similar experience to that evening at the nightclub when I was drugged and raped. I was finding my own voice, and when men got aggressive I simply removed myself from the situation.

And then there were the catfishers and oddballs. One guy had been chatting with me for weeks. Eventually, we decided to meet and I went over to his place. When he swung open the door, I saw the same guy from the photos, except those photos were obviously from a distant past. He was a nice enough man, but the attraction and chemistry just weren't there. It wasn't just the superficial fact that he was quite a bit older than advertised; it was that I felt I couldn't trust him since our first interactions were based on his lies. I didn't want to hurt his feelings, however. He had *Sex and the City* playing in the background and, though I had never watched a single minute of that show, I improvised and spent hours talking with him about it. I sat awkwardly on the edge of his sofa, as far away from him as possible, and made comments like, 'Oh, I just love how feisty Samantha is.' As the time ticked away, he started to yawn, and I used that as an excuse to leave. 'You know what? It's late and you're obviously tired, maybe tonight isn't the right time, but it was so good to meet you. Let's touch base later in the week and see how we feel!'

There was another guy who, when I arrived at his place, had episodes of *Dance Academy* playing on the television beside his bed. When he and I had been talking prior to our meeting, he hadn't let on that he knew who I was; however, upon arrival, he told me he was a big fan of mine, and of the show. While this was a compliment, it was just a bit weird. To top that off, he produced a box from under his bed filled with sex toys and said that it would be a dream come true for him to use them on me with the show playing in the background. Hard pass. This was really not my scene but as I tried to leave, he revealed that he was a casting director and would be able to get me more acting work. I, however, had never seen the value in sleeping my way to the top – I preferred to work based on ability and merit, rather than self-compromise.

I had a bit of a bad taste in my mouth from the men I had been meeting on these 'dating apps', so it was a refreshing change to be going on an old-school date with Ken, and I was excited to meet him.

***

He took me to a local Japanese restaurant and, let me tell you, that boy had some good taste. I hadn't realised until then but, as an armchair foodie myself, culinary appreciation was a very sexy quality. So too was film knowledge. I was no snob about it but, as it was a passion of mine, it was delightful to go toe-to-toe with him as we got to know each other through our film tastes. We had such a lively discussion that neither of us even noticed that the restaurant had cleared out, all of the other tables had been packed up, and the staff were not too subtly attempting to get us to leave. As we left he opened the door for me, which no-one had ever done before.

We went back to my apartment after dinner. Our intentions were only to watch a movie, I swear, but there was such chemistry sizzling between us that, soon, things started to get hot and heavy. But then, almost as soon as it had begun, Ken put his hand on my chest and gently pushed me away.

'No,' he said. 'I don't want to sleep with you. Sorry, that came out wrong. I just really like you, and I don't want to fuck it up.'

I felt so respected. An excitement I hadn't felt in a very long time, if ever, roared inside me.

It wasn't long before we were spending every day of the week together, though we didn't sleep together for several months. Ken worked near my apartment in Studio City but lived quite far away. In order for us to spend time together, he would come over after work. Due to the long distance home, he began spending the night. This became the daily routine almost immediately. It was definitely moving fast, but I had blinders on and couldn't remember when I had laughed so much on such a regular basis.

About a month into seeing each other, Ken went home to have dinner with his family, and when he returned the next day, he had all his clothing and possessions with him. His family were moving, and it seemed he was moving in with me. This wasn't something we had discussed, and I was pretty taken aback, to be honest. However, he had more or less been living with me already so I didn't make a big deal out of it, nor did I want to push him away. He piled his boxes in my bedroom, and I said nothing.

And yet there was that feeling again. This was all too soon. I didn't want the baggage of the last relationship to spoil what was so different and rewarding this time, but deep down I wondered if I was making the same mistake again. I certainly didn't think I was ready. But Ken was a different person. He wasn't fake like Liam. He had a job, could actually afford his car and was very attentive to my needs. So while there was a shadow of a doubt, I paid it no heed.

Ken's arrival, however, started to drive a wedge between me and my roommate, Russ, who had been a great friend to me in my darkest times. He felt taken advantage of and rightfully so, as Ken moving in was not something that had been discussed with him, either. Eventually, Russ and I talked about the financial split in the apartment. Ken and I had the larger room with the ensuite, and Ken was using one of the parking spots. Russ was willing to do an even three-way split, but Ken refused, only wanting to split my portion with me. I made the compromise, without telling Ken, that I would just pay Russ extra each month in order to keep the peace. The whole conversation caused Ken to dislike Russ intensely. The apartment, therefore, became a place where we would tiptoe around each other. The red flags were beginning to show, but I was reluctant to acknowledge them.

I'm truly ashamed of how I started to treat Russ. I took my partner's side and didn't do enough to discourage the animosity that was constantly bubbling away between them. This would have been particularly difficult for Russ, as I ended up travelling back and forth to Australia over the next couple of years for film shoots as well as some publicity appearances for *Red Billabong*, leaving Russ and Ken alone in the apartment together, constantly at each other's throats.

My first argument with Ken was about something that seemed so trivial to me. We had gone to watch a singer-songwriter friend perform a set at a bar in Hollywood called Vaucluse, directly opposite the Chateau Marmont. Though I had been 'out' for a couple of years now and had been introducing Ken to everyone as my boyfriend, I hadn't yet built up the comfort to hold hands in public. Any displays of affection around other people made me feel very uncomfortable. I had never been a very tactile person in the first place, but after so many years of conditioning myself to hate my 'same-sex attractions', something as simple as holding hands with another guy made every hair stand on end. Whenever he tried to slip his hand into mine, my body would automatically tense up, my breathing would become shallow, and a sudden flood of self-consciousness would immediately pull me out of whatever I was doing. I'd find it difficult to hold a conversation or keep my train of thought. Though I have come to understand, after years of therapy, that it was an anxiety issue caused by the negative feelings I'd had about my sexuality, back then I didn't have this awareness, much less the words to explain it to Ken. For him, it came across as personal. I had shared my life story with him so he knew where I was coming from, but on that night at the bar, he was constantly trying to hold my hand, even though he knew the irrational discomfort it caused me. I would politely rebuff him, expecting him to understand. However, on the drive home, he blew up at me. My friend's girlfriend had been sitting with us at the bar, and Ken felt like she was being flirty. He had wanted to take my hand as a way to mark his territory. He felt that I was trying to hide him or was ashamed to be seen with him. None of these things were the case at all and I was upset that he felt that way.

The truth of the matter was that it would have been far healthier for me in the long run if I had taken more time before dating again, especially after the tumultuous events of the year before. I needed more time to come to terms with myself. But we were now already living together and 'I love you's were already being exchanged.

I would do little things to try and show him that I was making an effort, like taking his hand when we went grocery shopping, or giving him random pecks when we socialised with friends.

This did come back to haunt me, however. After being at a friend's birthday party, I received a phone call from my Australian agent. One of his other clients had attended the same party and commented to my agent that she had seen me with my boyfriend. My agent didn't know I was gay and he was furious with me for apparently lying to him. While I didn't really see how it was any of his business, he was concerned about my castability. As ours was a business relationship in which he made money from the work I was cast in, I guess there was some validity to his concerns. It was he who had said, 'Gay guys don't get cast as leading men or superheroes.' He told me he would need to strategise around this new revelation, and his next call was to my American agents, to whom he outed me. Try as I might to rid myself of my homosexual shame, around every corner there were constant reminders.

For the most part, though, life with Ken was bliss for the first several months. Eventually, we started sleeping together. It felt like something I owed him, and something that was expected. And I felt I needed to reward his patience by finally allowing it to happen. I realised, however, that I still had such a negative relationship with sex. After the initial passion, my brain would suddenly sober out of the sexual pleasure I was in the middle of experiencing. I would think about my mum witnessing this from heaven. I would think about my soul. I would see that ghastly image of Satan from *The Exorcist* in my mind's eye. I would no longer be present in the sexual act or feel anything pleasurable from it. But, not wanting to ruin the experience for Ken, I used my acting skills to pretend that I was just as invested in the moment as he was. There was always a moment in the throes of passion when my mind would click and I'd go from pleasure to guilt in a heartbeat. It wasn't his fault, so I sold my performance. We'd giggle together in bed afterward, but when I was finally alone while he showered, I would be left with the demons in my head. I stared up at the ceiling and felt the full weight of my mum's disappointment in me and God's shame about who I had become and what I had just done. I had committed yet another mortal sin. It was unavoidable that my soul was destined for hell.

I did try to talk to Ken about this after a while, but he took it personally.

'Oh, so I don't actually exist as a person to you? I'm just a demon sent from hell to tempt you?' he said to me.

I understood what he was saying but thought that he was missing the point. I wasn't trying to put anything on him at all. I just wanted to communicate openly about what was going on in my head. I wanted him to understand me fully, and vice versa, so that we could always have each other's backs.

At the same time, though, I was also dealing with major trust issues. After the manipulation I had experienced at school, my mum's and sister's sneaky ambush tactics, my father's infidelity and, more recently, everything that had gone down with Liam, my trust reserves were low, and overthinking had become a survival mechanism. Ken was six years younger than me. When we first met, he was twenty-three and I was twenty-nine. He had been a typical frat boy in college and, prior to meeting me, had been single for a few years and was very used to being a man about town. I wondered if he was capable of hanging up his bachelor lifestyle and the freedom that came with it. I was scared that I was still too naive to spot any potential untrustworthy behaviour, as I had been duped so many times before by almost everyone I had ever loved. And I knew that there had been some red flags I had chosen to ignore.

Was I right to ignore them? There was one friend of his who I just had a weird feeling about, but I was also conscious of not becoming that crazy boyfriend accusing their partner of suspicious behaviour because of my own baggage. There were moments when I failed, however, and this guy was discussed a few times. Repeatedly denying unfounded accusations must have been exhausting. Ken always assured me that it was all in my head, and I was always mortified that I had blurted out my insecurities. But I was always looking over my shoulder, constantly expecting another curveball. So, in order to mitigate the damage, I was in a state of hypervigilance so that I could spot a threat a mile away and not be blindsided again.

However, a month later, Ken did something that made me feel more loved, seen and understood than I had ever felt before.

I was turning thirty in October, and on the first day of the month he woke me at 5 am.

'Babe, it's your birthday month!' he said. 'You've missed out on a lot in life.'

I blinked up at him in confusion. 'What?'

'I think you deserve to live life more and have some more experiences.'

'Okay?'

'We're going to do thirty "first things" for your thirtieth birthday. One each day until we tick them all off! Now come on, get up, we don't want to be late!'

'It's 5 am!'

'Yep. Day one. Disneyland. Let's go!'

I was floored. This was such a thoughtful gesture and I felt so seen. He had spent weeks planning this, all just for me, and I was overwhelmed by it. I didn't have the heart to tell him that I had already been to Disneyland when I was thirteen.

Over the course of the month, I fell deeper and deeper in love with him. I was ashamed for having doubted him. My walls came crumbling down, and I placed all my trust in him. What Liam and I had experienced was nowhere near 'love' if *this* was what it felt like. Some of the things on Ken's list of 'firsts' were extravagant, like Disneyland or meals out at expensive Hollywood restaurants, while others were cute in their simplicity, like sharing a milkshake together at an American diner. It was so lovely and cute of him, and I was so happy.

The month culminated in a party weekend in the Yucca Valley. Thirteen of my best friends rented a mansion in the middle of the desert. It was at the top of a hill, with 360-degree views, an infinity pool and a twenty-person jacuzzi. It was the best birthday I had ever had, and I was high on life.

A week later, we were at a Halloween party, gushing about the fabulous time we'd had. We went as WALL-E and EVE, and we were that nauseating couple who were the envy of everyone else in the room. When we got home, he was borderline blackout drunk. I popped him in the shower, still grinning from ear to ear about the month we'd just shared together and how truly blessed I was feeling. So much for God punishing me for being gay. After about half an hour, the shower was still running so I checked in on him to make sure he hadn't passed out, only to find him naked, taking racy photos of himself and sending them to someone.

I was not that someone.

It was a random guy we had met that night at the party. Right under my nose, they had swapped numbers and started sexting each other while still at the party.

So there it was. The other shoe had finally dropped.

In the argument that ensued, Ken admitted that the guy I *had* been worried about for months was, in fact, someone I *should* have been worried about all along. Not only did they have a history together, but they had been sharing similar content with each other throughout the entirety of our relationship.

The joy and happiness of the past month disintegrated in an instant. When he woke up the next morning, he had forgotten all about it due to his level of intoxication, so we had to have the conversation a second time around, which was fun.

With the rug pulled out from underneath me, I was in a daze. Ken was very remorseful, and I couldn't help but feel sorry for him, for how miserable he was. I was miserable, too. I didn't want to lose him. I had invested so much into the relationship already and I didn't want to feel the way I had when I broke up with Liam. Though I didn't just forgive him immediately and sweep it under the rug, like I had with Liam, I did believe in him and in us and I asked for some time to think things over. He spent the next few weeks going above and beyond for me, which I guess is exactly what a cheater would do when they're caught, but I took it for genuine contrition. But just three weeks later, while we were still trying to figure things out, I had to fly to Australia to shoot another film for a month.

We had moved so fast in our relationship, and I should have learned my lesson from the last one. While I wasn't punishing him for what happened, I wasn't going to rush any decisions. I needed time and separation so I could reflect. Being away for a few weeks to shoot the movie was the perfect opportunity for this and would allow me to think more clearly.

I won't mention the name of the film that I shot, as it is something that never saw the light of day. I believe a version of it does exist now, though it no longer resembles the project that I signed up for. It had an interesting and unique premise, and was in the young-adult fiction genre that had become the cultural craze at the time. It also reunited me with actors who I had known from other projects, like my sister from another mister, Alicia Banit from *Dance Academy*, and Nikolai Nikolaeff and Christopher Kirby from *Camp*. Though the film had a host of production issues, it was a fun time. The cast all lived together in a beautiful house in the middle of a Queensland rainforest, and we got to shoot some really cool scenes in some stunning locations, wearing out-of-this-world costumes. It's a shame that the film wasn't completed as scripted because I truly believed in the story. It had taken me into territory that, as an actor, I hadn't had the opportunity to explore before, and I really enjoyed the creative fulfilment it provided.

A lot of people don't realise that it is very common for a TV or film production to collapse. The hard work of all the people involved goes to waste, and nothing ever comes of it. I'd had a taste of that on *Red Billabong*, but at least they were able to eventually complete the film and release it worldwide. This was my first – and only – experience where the entire thing went belly up and I really regretted that it didn't get its chance to prove itself.

It had, however, been an amazing opportunity to re-evaluate after the last few months with Ken. Being on set and doing what I loved always made me feel very connected to myself. And having the separation gave me enough time to reflect on our relationship, and what I deserved as a person.

By the end of the filming, I decided that I would continue my relationship with Ken, albeit proceeding with caution. He knew my feelings about what had happened and, because I had expressed those feelings, I felt like I had stood up for myself for the first time in my life. My belief was that we would start fresh once I got back to LA at the end of the shoot and, with a greater understanding of each other, the relationship could end up stronger.

The film wrapped production just a couple of days before Christmas. I could have stayed in Australia for Christmas with my family, but I still felt icky about my dad's situation and my relationship with my sister had only crumbled further. A family Christmas was therefore not an enticing option. I decided, instead, to return to Los Angeles with my Aussie actor friends, who were also spending the holiday away from their families. A huge Christmas Eve celebration was organised at a friend's house the day I was landing back, and I was excited to spend the festive season with my chosen family.

I boarded a plane back to Los Angeles, fully prepared to start things anew with Ken and see where it took me. Right before my flight, he texted me saying that I should wear something nice when I arrived in LA. He said he had a surprise for me and I needed to be dressed up for it. I bought a new suit and shirt, intrigued by what he had in store.

Once I had landed, I got myself all dolled up and ventured out into the arrivals hall. Ken was standing there wearing a beautiful suit in royal blue, my favourite colour. He looked gorgeous.

Suddenly, he was down on one knee, an open ring box in his hand.

I ... didn't know what to think. I had never thought I would ever get married, let alone under circumstances like these. It had been less than two months since I had discovered his infidelity and we had only spent three of those weeks together trying to salvage our relationship. My intention was to start over, not take the plunge into the deep end. And yet we were at the international arrivals hall on Christmas Eve, with hundreds of onlookers cheering us on. Out of the crowd stepped Ken's friend Rebecca, filming the proposal on her phone. And we were literally driving straight from the airport to our friends' Christmas Eve party. I'm not sure if anyone else can relate to the feeling of having so many thoughts in your brain that they cancel each other out and you're left with no thoughts at all? Well, that's how I felt. It was too much to process all at once, and I felt nothing. But with the cheering crowd, the friend filming, our existing Christmas plans and the fact that I had no other options in that moment, this didn't feel like the right time to say no ...

So I said yes.

***

Another mistake. I was simply too weak and immature to make the braver decision. I thought, naively, that we would exult in the joys of our engagement over the festive period and then we could have a serious discussion about where we *actually* were once we settled into the new year.

Ken held my hand during the entire car ride from the airport while he called all his family members and friends to tell them the exciting news on speaker. It makes me sad to admit it, but I wasn't happy at all in those moments. I felt numb and alone.

An engagement is meant to be the happiest day of someone's life, outside of the actual wedding day itself. And yet, once again, I was feeling cornered and trapped in my own mind.

Over the next couple of weeks, with all the Christmas and New Year's parties, we were surrounded by friends who were ecstatic about our news. We even flew to Australia (Ken's first time) and I introduced him to my dad and his wife, though they did insist that we sleep in separate bedrooms while we stayed with them. I have to admit that I got caught up in the romance and love of it all, and Ken was being so affectionate during this time. My conviction that I would talk with him about the engagement started to wane, and I kept putting off bringing it up with him. I even tried to introduce him to my sister. I made plans for us to spend a night in the Blue Mountains near her house and told her more than two months prior to the trip that I would like to make introductions. Rather than saying no, she kept giving me vague reasons as to why any of the proposed dates to meet up might not work for her. Over the three-day period that I was in her area, she stopped responding to me. Afterward, she told me she had just been too busy that week. But in arguments since, she has asked me why I would have expected her to meet my gay lover in the first place. 'You know I can't support this, Tim,' she said. But it really hurt my feelings that my sister didn't at least want to make sure I was in safe hands with the person I was committing to sharing a life with.

But though I had been somewhat swept up in the romantic fantasy, one thing that had really been weighing on my mind was how little time I had spent free. I had been out of the closet for all of two years, yet had spent eighteen months of that time in relationships that had both been problematic. In the remaining six months, though I'd had a handful of 'moments' with some men, I hadn't gone out on dates or spent any time trying to meet people at bars or clubs. I didn't even have any gay friends. I was starting to regret that I had exited my twenties without the chance to live them. I wished I had come out earlier, so that I could have enjoyed the coming of age that the twenties provide. I craved the ability to find solace with myself.

I should have been honest with Ken that I had started to feel trapped again, and I underestimated just how strong that feeling would become. As much as it would have hurt me if we did end up breaking up, it would have been the right thing to do for both of us. It wasn't fair of me to string him along, even though that's not how I viewed it at the time. I was essentially setting the stage for what eventually became a very toxic and controlling relationship, so I have to take my share of the blame. I was being a coward.

Ken could sense that I was preoccupied. It was bound to have come across as me pulling away. He tried hard to break through. One day, he adopted a couple of cats for me, thinking they would bring me some joy, which they did.

We named them London and Olive, and though I hadn't been a cat person until then, I fell in love with them instantly. Every so often, he would find cheap hotel stays and take me out of town for quick weekend getaways, and surprise me with tickets to see live orchestras at the Hollywood Bowl. He was a very sweet and attentive man, and a truly amazing gift-giver. But he was also controlling.

I had started to realise that I was a relationship chameleon, in the sense that I always morphed into a slightly different person based on who my partner was and what would make them happy. This had obviously started when I was a kid and needed to present myself in the family home in a way that was acceptable to the people I hoped to receive love from. It makes sense that this behaviour transitioned into how I approached my love life. Why had I pretended to want to do karaoke five times a week? Because Liam loved that. Why had I pretended to enjoy the TV show *Revenge*? Because it was Liam's favourite. Why had I attended all-night religious vigils to pray for all the sinful souls attending the Sydney Gay and Lesbian Mardi Gras when I was growing up? Because that was what Mum had wanted. My therapist's words about co-dependency started to finally make sense. When it came to Ken, I had suddenly become a huge fan of Nicki Minaj, because she was his number one. I had even bought us tickets to see her show. Ken also loved going to swanky Hollywood nightclubs where his best friend was a 'bottle girl', and so that became my favourite thing to do. I betrayed my good friend Russ because Ken didn't like him. But my behaviours also affected deeper things like the treatment I would put up with, and the issues to which I turned a blind eye. I knew I needed to be more independent, and I tried to start. But as Ken started noticing my growing self-sufficiency, he took it as a threat. His reaction to that was to become controlling.

He started to pull away himself and began behaving drastically differently. And so began a toxic cycle between the two of us. One was always chasing after the other. There'd be a few weeks of arguments and tears, followed by making up, cute romantic dates and a few weeks of happiness. Then the other one would start pulling away, another argument would ensue, accusations were levelled, and then cue another two weeks of misery followed by another two weeks of romantically making up.

I eventually made it clear to Ken that, unlike him, I had still yet to experience life as a confident gay man. It had only been through my relationships that I had started to build up my own personal acceptance of who I was, and I had never had a chance to experience how it felt to simply be me, without the expectations of others. I wanted to know what it felt like to just be my big gay self, to not be ashamed if a cute guy at the gym approached me, to flirt without feeling that it was wrong. I needed to feel free. What I really needed was to be single. But my stupid loneliness got in the way and I selfishly didn't want to lose him. So, in among all that chaos, we stupidly decided to try the whole 'open relationship' thing.

It was about a year after our engagement. I eventually opened up fully about how I had been feeling. Being so sheltered and repressed for such a long time meant that I had only just begun to come into my own. As I continued to discover more about myself, changes in what I personally needed were inevitable.

'I'm jealous of you,' I said.

'Why?' he asked.

'You had a supportive family. You were allowed to be confident in yourself at a younger age. Explore yourself, explore your sexuality, enjoy the single life.'

'So you want to be single?' he said, anger and hurt in his eyes.

'No … sometimes … I don't know.' I trailed off feebly.

'Sounds like you do.'

I paused for a moment. 'I just want the freedom to be … me.'

He took his engagement ring off and slammed it on the bedside table. 'Fine. Go be free.'

I was conflicted, since I didn't want to break up with him, either. I did love him. 'I just want a taste,' I said.

'No, you want to have your cake and eat it, too. You want me to be your crutch. Fine. We'll open things up. But I won't put up with double standards – you get to do your thing, I get to do mine!'

Ultimately, Ken was right. I did want a taste of freedom but was too scared to be alone. This was wrong of me. And it was unfair to him. A part of me thought that it could bring us closer together because of the level of honesty it would require. But, for me, it wasn't even really about sex; it was about things as simple as being flirtatious. I had barely ever flirted in my life because I was always hiding my sexuality. If a guy caught me checking him out in the gym mirror, rather than looking away in guilt and fear, I wanted to experience the confidence of maintaining eye contact. I wanted to put an end to my personal stigma against gay nightclubs because of the experience I had back in 2013. I wanted to venture out more. Maybe even kiss a boy on the dance floor. Essentially, just experience life a little, untethered by guilt. I could feel myself yearning for that moment when I would finally relax into myself. But the pressure of the engagement made me feel that I would never find closure for my unresolved regrets and resentments. And I feared that that moment of finally letting go of the negative energy of my past, and finding true acceptance of myself, might never happen. It wouldn't be right to marry someone still feeling that way, because then I would forever be trapped.

We decided to stay together but call off the engagement for the moment. However, we never told anyone and I never removed my engagement ring, so who were we kidding? For a brief period, our relationship improved but, ultimately, the great open relationship experiment didn't work for us. I knew he was going off and doing his thing from time to time, but I tried not to pay too much attention to it and didn't want to hold it against him. As for me, I was working four jobs seven days a week, so never had much opportunity to do anything, and he was monitoring me like a hawk. He paid close attention to my social media and my every move.

When I posted a photo of my new acting headshot on socials, he commented, 'And the thirsty DM slides begin in 3, 2, 1 ...' He then looked up any person who had liked or commented on it and made me answer for each of them. It didn't matter to him if the comment came from a fifteen-year-old girl in the Dominican Republic saying, 'OMG, I love you so much, Ethan', a reference to my character on *Dance Academy*. This was a threat to him, and he couldn't handle it. He started going to the gym at the same time as me instead of sticking to his usual routine, and even started showing up at my work while I was on shift so that he could monitor me. Not only was he the one who was actually making use of our agreement while I was prevented by my work obligations, but this was the opposite of the freedom I needed, and our fights became loud and frequent. The surveillance was reminiscent of what I had felt during my school years.

My roommate Russ, who had supported me and been such a kind friend over the years, moved out. Apart from Ken's ice-cold demeanour around him for years now, he was sick of the constant arguments. The stress of everything had started to change me, and I didn't treat Russ very fairly. I don't blame him for not wanting to be around Ken and my toxicity, but I'm ashamed of how I acted. This 'search for freedom' had resulted in the exact opposite. All Ken and I were doing was hurting each other's feelings. But now it had started to affect my friendships.

My other friends, too, began to pull back. I had become that person who refused to leave a bad relationship, but whose only topic of conversation was to complain about it. They had been witness to some of our arguments over the years, and they just didn't want to be involved in any of it, which I now completely understand. But without the support of friends or family, who else did I have? No-one. And that kept me glued to Ken for years.

This entire period also collapsed the professional relationships I had built up over the years. While all this gay drama was unfurling, my Australian agent and I parted ways suddenly. We'd had a disagreement about some changes I had been wanting to make with my American representation. I hadn't felt like the opportunities coming my way were realistic. I had therefore wanted to address how best to move forward and thought that maybe a shift in representation could help. This, however, didn't work out. Though I had an Australian agent, an American agent and an American talent manager working on my team, I had taken some meetings behind their backs to see if someone else might be able to position me better in the industry. Unfortunately, however, it is quite a small industry, and word got out that I was seeking new representation. The meetings I had organised ended up not working out, but word had reached my existing reps that I was shopping around. My Australian agent called to tell me that I had failed in the game of chess I was apparently playing. As I was on such a downward spiral at the time, I allowed the conversation to get heated and lost professionalism for a moment. My agent, mind you, was an absolute pitbull so he wasn't blameless here, either. We yelled at each other over the phone for thirty minutes, and just like that, my entire team of agents and managers, both in Australia and the US, was gone. Ironically, this happened just moments before the Los Angeles premiere of *Red Billabong*. Shortly after ending the shouting match with my agent, I had to step out in front of an audience and introduce the movie and the creative team behind it. It took every ounce of acting ability for me to put on a brave face and pretend like everything was fine despite knowing that I had just ruined my career. And so, as we watched the movie, all I could think about was that everything I had worked so hard to achieve had crumbled around me.

I had once again hit the bottom rung of the worst time in my life. I felt like I was having a complete mental breakdown. I hopped on a plane to Australia to escape Los Angeles and the life I had been living. It had been five years since I had come out and yet the demons were just as loud as ever. My default setting was to assume that all these negative setbacks were God's punishment. I deserved them.

I was angry with the world and with my circumstances. Everything was such a massive struggle, and the setbacks were always so extreme. I was angry about what had happened to my family, and still had so many unresolved issues with them. And I realised I needed to find a way to let go of everything in order to move on. And the only way to do that was to address them.

I started by somehow giving religion one more chance.

While in Australia, I reached out to an old school friend. He was the Franciscan priest with whom I had led the children's choir a few years earlier. I came out to him and shared my recent struggles. He invited me to the church to catch up. I hoped that his prior friendship and knowledge of me would inspire a more compassionate response to what I was dealing with. Instead, we sat in his office and he put on a recorded lecture by an American bishop titled 'The Destructive Nature of Homosexuality'.

I gripped the armrests of the chair while I sat in silence and listened with him. When the recording ended, I didn't say much. He asked me, 'How do you feel?'

And I replied, 'Worse.'

As I left his office he gifted me a copy of the lecture we had just listened to, in case I needed its guidance moving forward. So kind of him.

I knew in that moment that I was wasting my time with my religion and the Opus Dei world I had grown up in. It was so clear now how ridiculous it was for me to expect that I would ever get a reasoned, respectful and empathetic understanding from anyone from the religious part of my life, because they were too rigid in their opinions and incapable of hearing a dissenting voice. It was good to get confirmation on this. I could let go of that expectation.

My dad and his wife picked me up afterward. I sat in silence the whole way home. It had become clear to me that I would never receive the understanding I was searching for from my religious community, and therefore the next thing I needed to let go of was the resentment I had held toward my dad and his wife over the years.

After he parked the car, I told Dad that we needed to have a chat.

It was a dark night. The clouds hung low, covering the tree-lined country road in a cold, damp mist. We shivered as we walked down the creepy avenue. The fog lay over the ground and trees swayed ominously in the breeze.

'Dad, I know you two were seeing each other while Mum was alive,' I blurted out.

Dad's pace slowed. 'And how do you know that?' he asked.

'You backed up your mobile phone onto the family computer,' I said.

'I see,' said Dad, always a man of few words.

'Look, Dad, I get it. I think you guys are way more suited for each other than you and Mum ever were,' I continued. 'But I hope you understand how hurtful it was to find out. It's kinda hypocritical that I'm considered the bad guy in the family when the sin I'm supposedly guilty of never came at anyone's expense.'

He nodded slowly, not looking at me. 'I see your point,' he said at last. 'We called it off when your mother got sick, though.'

'Whatever,' I said, sceptical. 'Look, at the end of the day, I'm glad you're happy now. But I think I'm entitled to the same happiness as you. I'm sick of being made to feel guilty by everyone because of something I never asked for and tried so hard to ignore.'

'Who's making you feel guilty?' he asked.

I laughed bitterly. 'Come on, Dad. You know how I grew up.'

Dad sighed. 'Well, it's your life now. You can do whatever you want.'

We had never been a father-and-son duo who had deep life chats, so we were both out of our element here, but this was the deepest conversation I had ever had with him. Some of the resentment I'd held onto for so many years started to wash away. We were freezing and the wind began to kick up.

'Is that what you wanted to tell me?' he asked.

'Pretty much,' I replied. And we headed back to the house.

When I returned to the house, my godmother was sitting in front of the bristling fireplace.

Before I could say 'now it's your turn', she pre-empted me and said, 'So, you know.'

She acknowledged the affair, despite downplaying her part in it. And she affirmed her commitment to my dad and our family. She made it clear that no family is perfect, and each has its own issues, but that whatever had transpired, they would always be there for me. As I went to bed that night, I felt lighter. I had gained a small sense of closure. And I couldn't deny that she and my dad had, like she'd said, always supported me (which was not something I could have guaranteed if my mother was still around!). And I no longer had to hold onto the secret I had kept for her and my dad all these years.

Though these were all positive steps toward shaking off the troubles that had kept me living in the past, I shortly returned to Los Angeles and picked up the pieces of my relationship with Ken. I had faith that we could continue to learn and grow together and that it would all work out in the end. But sadly, over the next eighteen months, we reverted back to the same old toxic cycle. Our co-dependency ensured that no matter how bad things got, we would always end up together. I loved him so much, and the good days were amazing. But I was always walking on eggshells around him, never knowing which version of him I was going to get. It was so exhausting, and I simply didn't have the time to always pander to his needs. So in the interests of my new self-improvement journey, I put my focus on fixing my finances and become who I really was.

By the end of 2019, I received a promotion at the swanky Hollywood bar I had been working at. The significant pay rise this represented, as well as the savings I had made, meant that I was able to save up for my next visa and contemplate travelling to the UK to finally meet my biological brother in person. We had remained in constant contact over the past decade but still hadn't had the chance to actually meet.

Though it made me sad to think it, despite how much I loved him, I was starting to feel that Ken and I had done irreparable damage to our relationship and were fooling ourselves by staying together. I would find myself daydreaming of living somewhere else, being single and having a chance to reinvent myself. I was still craving freedom, and I knew that a large part of myself had felt trapped by the relationship. It felt eerily close to how I had felt when I was at home with my mother monitoring my every move. I needed time to figure things out on my own. Unfortunately, it was becoming all too clear that I needed to do the next part of my learning alone. But I was too scared to admit it.

CHAPTER THIRTEEN

Born-Again Version

I had a good feeling about 2020. At the same time, I distrusted my sense of optimism and wondered if something was about to go drastically wrong. My life had trained me to expect the unexpected, and I had grown to learn that contentment was always met with a downfall – like a block of Jenga that could be toppled at a moment's notice.

Since moving to Los Angeles seven years prior, I had had a pretty rough time of it and had stumbled my way through major obstacles in my dogged pursuit of success. Not just success as an actor, but as a person. With so many people in my life criticising every choice I made, whether that be my career or my relationships, I was hyper-focused on proving to myself, just as much as anyone else, that I wasn't wrong in wanting to be myself and that I could find fulfilment in my career as well as with a partner.

My paranoia, however, only went so far as to worry that the bar I worked for would make me redundant. I thought that perhaps there would be another death in the family or that I, myself, would succumb to some sort of illness – a very real fear for an adopted kid in his mid-thirties with precious little information about any genetic illnesses that I should be on the lookout for. Doctors always asked if there's a history of things like cancer in the family, and while I would respond that my mother died of cancer, I would also have to clarify that she wasn't my biological mother and that I had no idea if I was predisposed to anything of note. But, as it turned out, any of those worries were trivial compared to what actually happened.

The COVID-19 pandemic claimed millions of lives, levelled economies and brought the world to its knees. It threw everyone into complete chaos and had devastating effects on billions of people. One friend in Los Angeles had a father who was desperately awaiting a kidney transplant. Right before the pandemic hit, he was offered the opportunity to take part in a promising new trial that could save his life. He opted to participate, taking him off the kidney transplant registry. When the pandemic hit, the experimental treatment he was in line for was shelved and he was no longer in the queue to receive a kidney. As his life started to drain away during the first wave of the virus, his own daughter couldn't even visit him in the last months of his life. Instead, she could only drive to his house and sit on his front lawn while he stayed inside and looked at her through his living room window. A few weeks later, he died.

Another friend's father suffered a heart attack. My friend flew from London to Sydney to spend the last days of his father's life with him but was only granted one hour to see him before his passing, and had no choice but to accommodate the harsh restrictions in place for the funeral service.

These are just two situations that I am personally privy to. There are countless more stories indicative of COVID-19's devastating impact around the globe.

In the scheme of things, any of the hardships that I endured pale in comparison to these tales. I know that I had it easy, under the circumstances. So even though it felt like the worst possible thing at the time, I know that it wasn't and, in fact, the forced period of change that the pandemic dragged me into, kicking and screaming, ended up as the greatest blessing in disguise.

In February 2020, Los Angeles joined much of the world in lockdown, and my job was no more. As I was on a working visa in the US, I wasn't able to claim any government benefits and, having just paid another huge fee to reside legally in the country, my savings were once again very dry. I wouldn't be able to go without work for long and just had to hope, with blind optimism, that it would all blow over soon.

The political unrest in America at the time provided additional apocalyptic flare. The Trump v. Biden 2020 election was happening, the Black Lives Matter protests were taking place, and all the closed businesses and shops were being boarded up with wood. Cop cars were set ablaze within metres of my house, the shops were being looted, people were brawling in grocery store parking lots over toilet paper and stocking up on canned goods, and the queues of people lining up outside gun and ammunition stores stretched for blocks.

One day, Ken and I drove through Hollywood, just as an escape from our four walls, and saw dozens of military tanks and hundreds of fully uniformed troops with guns at the ready, all standing in formation along Hollywood Boulevard. It was a scary sight, and made it the worst time to watch Steven Soderbergh's *Contagion*, as the film now had a chilling documentary-like feel.

Ken and I isolated together. Over the next few months, while we hopefully waited for the pandemic to end, he and I grew closer than we had been in years. Without the distractions of the outside world, when it was just the two of us, things were calm and we relied on each other to get through the turmoil of what was happening around us.

By mid-2020, however, my money was running out; the Australian consulate in Los Angeles was closing its doors, the flights to Australia were being drastically reduced, and it was announced that, soon, anyone returning to Australia would be charged several thousand dollars for a mandatory two-week quarantine period. If I chose to stay in LA, with no money and no form of income, I would end up a drain on Ken's own resources and I didn't want to ruin our relationship that way. I would have felt like Liam. I also couldn't afford paying a hefty fee for a flight home and the quarantine period. If I didn't leave in that moment, I would become the burden of all burdens, which was something I had tried to avoid being my whole life.

I had to make the difficult decision to leave. I had a conversation with my dad and his wife one night. They brought the reality home to me. I had no choice. I had to give up the life I had sacrificed so much for. When I hung up the phone, I collapsed onto the living room couch. Ken sat beside me and rubbed my back while I cried inconsolably. Though I had tried everything I could to make my life in LA work, it was time to admit defeat. A flight was booked, and I packed not even a quarter of my belongings, wishfully thinking that I would be back within a couple of months.

The day Ken took me to the airport was the single hardest day of my life. After collecting my ticket and checking my bags, we sat in the departure hall together for half an hour. We didn't speak. We just sat together and held each other. I didn't want to leave him. Though we weren't breaking up, and hoped that our separation would only last a brief few months while the world righted itself, it still *felt* like a break-up. I was hysterically inconsolable while I experienced the overwhelming feeling that I wasn't going to see him again. Deep down, I knew that it was right for both of us not to be together, but it felt like the death of a loved one. Having experienced that, it was a profound feeling.

When it inevitably came time for me to head to the security gate, I gave him one last, long hug and told him to please not look back at me as I went up the escalators. I, however, broke my own rule, and when I looked back, he was standing there looking up at me as the escalator took me further and further away. I gestured for him to walk away, and the last that I saw of him, in his pink tank top with tears streaming from his eyes, was his body turning the corner and vanishing behind a pillar, out of sight. I never saw him again.

It was more than heartbreak; I simply felt empty. Despite the multiple rough patches, the good times always outweighed the bad, and my relationship with him had made me feel more seen and valid than any other in my life. We had been through a lot together and had fought a long and hard battle to stay in each other's lives. Utterly co-dependent, we had been each other's worlds for more than five years. Despite us calling off our engagement, I had still considered myself engaged to him. But now, it was all over, along with the Hollywood dreams that I had worked so hard to keep alive. The past seven years of struggle, growth, tenacity, self-belief and hanging onto hope felt like they had imploded. And everything about who I was, what I wanted and what I had worked to achieve had left me with nothing.

The flight was a surreal experience. Everyone on the plane, including the cabin crew and pilots, had the same look of stifled panic in their eyes – we were all sharing the same trauma, with an unknown world waiting for us on the other end of the flight. Like me, most people were too anxious or upset to be distracted by the in-flight entertainment. We all sat in silence as we hurtled through the air, trying our best not to melt down at the sheer weight of the unknown.

When our flight landed, we were greeted by medical personnel in full protective gear. We were tested and then handed over to the army, who escorted us into huge warehouses, where we were sat in chairs spaced several metres apart. We were left waiting for hours. Eventually, we were marshalled by the army and police officers onto buses and taken to mystery locations. The bus driver didn't even know where we would end up. He just had to follow the police escort he had been provided with. Upon arrival at the quarantine facility, we were processed and escorted one by one to our rooms, where we were left in complete isolation for two weeks.

Thankfully, I was taken to a very nice hotel for my quarantine. While, obviously, all of the hotel amenities were off limits, as I couldn't leave my room, it was a very comfortable space and, three times a day, a knock on the door would signal that a meal had been delivered. It would often be a cold omelette or cold curry, and we had no choice but to be grateful for the provisions. I had never had to check my privilege so much, and needed to keep my complaints in line.

While sequestered in my room for two weeks, I would talk with Ken for hours each day and spend the rest of my time playing the piano keyboard that I had brought with me, or watching news stories unfold about all the people refusing to adhere to social distancing or mask mandates. I would sit for hours at my window, which overlooked a construction site that still had work being done on it. I made up names and backstories for the workers I would see. One day, I saw an argument between two of them and decided that Jarrod (as I called him) and Michael (he looked like a Michael) had slept with each other's girlfriends but were now forced to work together in this dwindling economy. I lapped up the imagined drama that their life outside my prison provided.

One night, a disturbance in the hall outside my room broke out. I stood, glued to the peephole on my door, watching soldiers, police and ambulance personnel rushing up and down the hallway outside. A woman in an adjacent room had suffered a psychotic break while in quarantine and had tried to throw a chair through the hotel window – perhaps an attempt to escape, or maybe just to get some fresh air. Her partner had tried to placate her, but she had grabbed a shard of glass from the broken window and had injured him with it. There was some confusion about what to do in this situation, as they were both in quarantine, but after hours of deliberation, the police broke into the room, sedated the woman, took her away and provided medical assistance to her partner. It felt wrong to witness all this, and for it to be the only source of entertainment we had, but that was what life had been reduced to. The rest of the time in quarantine was a jet-lagged fever dream of digging up the past and wondering how everything that had happened in life had led to this moment of such utter powerlessness.

After fourteen days and nights secluded in that room, with nothing but my negative thoughts to occupy me, I was eventually released. Stepping out into fresh air, being able to see the blue of the sky and the brilliance of the sunshine, was a profoundly emotional experience. I had never smiled at the blue sky before, or noticed just how much I enjoyed the feeling of fresh crisp air filling my nasal cavities. I understood the privilege of my life the moment I had an emotional reaction to simply breathing fresh air and seeing the sunlight after two weeks in solitary confinement.

My dad had driven two hours to come and collect me. It was such a kind gesture and it was my first time seeing him in years. I spent the next six months living with him and his wife in their beautiful cottage in country New South Wales. Though I had made peace with their marriage at this point, it still felt awkward to be in my mid-thirties and living with them after I had tried so hard to set my own life up for myself and avoid the strangeness of what my family had become. But I also started to feel guilty about the amount of resentment and animosity I had felt toward them over the years. They had proven themselves time and time again to be supportive and caring of me. I had allowed so many years of being caught up in the injustice of their past actions to jeopardise that. They had saved me and were incredibly understanding and gentle with me while I was, once more, starting all over again.

Their home was located down a long, tranquil country road. I spent days walking around the gorgeous countryside listening to music and podcasts. The restrictions in their town were less extreme, due to the location and population size of the area, and so I was able to spend time at the gym and swim for a few hours each day. I spent my evenings locked in my room writing music and would only emerge when my dad and his wife were done with their days. I wanted to cause as little disruption to their lives as possible while going through this upheaval. Though it gave me the time I needed to think, it was a very isolating period, and it was difficult to justify the strides I thought I had made, with the results that life was currently offering.

Dad and his wife were patient and understanding with me while I navigated this new world and fresh start. I don't think that I've communicated enough to them just how grateful I am for that. I really was an entitled, privileged spoiled brat. Having said that, it was difficult to be in my bedroom at their place and overhear their night-time bedroom tickle fights. But the grudge that I had carried for so many years didn't serve anyone anymore, least of all me. Reality couldn't be changed and I couldn't fault them for the efforts they were making, and the love and support they were giving me. I wouldn't be where I am today without them.

After six months of living with them, it became clear that my 'couple of months' of living in Australia before returning to America was out of the question. Not only had the Australian government made it virtually impossible for people to leave the country during the pandemic, but I simply didn't have the funds to support returning to a life over there. So, no matter how begrudgingly, I made peace with the fact that Australia was where I now called home.

I found an apartment in Sydney and, not wanting to be a drain on the taxpayer, started to work some really horrible jobs to make ends meet. For a time, I worked in a call centre that was scamming vulnerable people out of money with the promise that their funds were going to charities. Dozens of us would sit in cubicles with prepared scripts and our phone lines would automatically connect us with people whose numbers were randomly generated through the company's database of unsuspecting victims. We would launch into our script and try to sell them on the benefits their charitable donations would achieve. For the most part, we would get hung up on. Often, we would get verbally abused for being scammers, and every now and then, we would find someone who bought into what the script was saying and then we'd press them for more and more money.

None of this sat well with my morals. I questioned the validity of what our supervisors were telling us about how the supposed charitable donations worked, or whether any money even went to the charities we were apparently calling on behalf of. But the Australian government didn't care about any of that. They just wanted to make sure that all the people displaced by the pandemic weren't just mooching off their unemployment benefits. I had rent and electricity bills to pay, and didn't want to feel like I was taking advantage of the system. So, for the time being, I needed this job.

However, the final straw came when I had a lengthy conversation with an elderly woman with three dogs. I had called 'on behalf' of an animal welfare charity and had spoken at length with the ageing woman about the need for funds to help abandoned pets and strays. She had told me that her pension barely allowed her to feed her three existing dogs and, therefore, she didn't have a cent to spare for the charitable cause I was supposedly representing. I had accepted this, as she sounded like a sweet and genuine person, and I ended the call. I was immediately brought into the boss's office to be reprimanded for letting her off the hook. They were listening in on every call, and to them, this represented my inability to close a deal and pump her for as much money as possible. I couldn't make any excuses, as I thought what they were doing was evil. I took the bad feedback. I took the hits. And fifteen minutes later, I told my boss I wasn't feeling well and needed the rest of the day off. As I was driving home, I called him to tell him I would no longer be working there anymore.

Instead, I took a job working in a supermarket, preparing samples of products on sale. I had to wear a chef's hat and apron, and set up station in high-traffic areas of supermarkets around Sydney so as to promote the product I was sampling. Every now and then, people would recognise me from *Dance Academy* or *X-Men* and want a photo with me. It felt like a constant reminder of how far I had fallen. 'What are you doing here?' they would ask. 'Why is this your job?' and I would just have to laugh and pretend that I was okay with this being my situation. But bills had to be paid, and I had to get over myself and be grateful for what I had. I soon found a better job working for a fitness club so I could avoid such soul-crushing questions. However, not long after I started working there, we entered another several months of lockdown.

Sydney felt like a foreign city to me; the majority of my friends lived overseas, I was barely scraping together enough money to pay the most basic of my bills, there was no social scene for meeting new people due to the COVID-19 restrictions, and now we were all shut-ins again, with strict limitations on the time we were allowed to spend outdoors and how far we could go from our home addresses. I was completely alone.

It was during this second lockdown that Ken and I broke off all communication. His life had bounced back to relative normality only a month or so after I had left, as Australia was being far stricter than the US in its handling of the pandemic. We had stayed in constant contact for an entire year after I left, but as it became clearer that I wouldn't be able to return to him, the tone of his conversations changed. He went from talking about plans together when I returned to the US to telling me stories about his sex life and dating experiences with other people. It hurt to hear these things, but I had no other option but to accept them. For me, however, it had been difficult to meet people during the brief time between lockdowns. But I had started to make some new friendships, and had even been brave enough to meet some people on dating apps. However, if I ever mentioned the names of the people I was meeting and the attempts I was making to move on in the same way that he was, I would be met with passive-aggressive insults and insinuations. If I mentioned the name of a guy, even if it was just a platonic friendship, Ken would find their social profiles, send me their photos and say things like, 'He's hot, hope you guys are very happy together.' He was still monitoring my every move while tormenting me with graphic descriptions of his own wild sex life.

It was time to cut things off. I didn't need more guilt in my life. It had already made me feel terrible to even try to put myself out there, because any time I would find myself even remotely interested in someone else, it felt like cheating. I also knew I didn't have it in me to fall for anyone just yet, and I'm pretty sure I pissed a lot of people off during that time as I became a huge flake. I was all talk and no follow-through, because I simply could never bring myself to open up to another person. My mental health had suffered a great deal. I had been leaning too heavily on Ken for emotional support, which wasn't fair of me. Even though an ocean separated us, we were still being just as toxic for one another. As difficult as it was, Ken and I agreed to leave each other alone and take the space we needed to get over each other. I hadn't wanted that, but it was for the best.

This meant that I finally had a chance to experience those missing rite-of-passage moments that I had been robbed of in my twenties. All those years of me daydreaming about a version of myself where I would live freely as myself had finally arrived in the most unlikely of ways. It was now time to embrace that freedom. I knew it wouldn't be easy, however – there would be more stumbles and lonely nights – but I was ready to let go of the past and get life back on track.

Once that second lockdown finally lifted, I was determined to make the most of my freedom. I met a lot of people during this time, and started to develop a new appreciation for how beautiful humanity could be. There is so much love and support in the world if only we open our eyes enough to see it.

My new friend Ryan, who had started out as a failed Tinder date, turned out to be one of the best friends and biggest supports I had ever had. He was so conscious of my mental health, provided me with much-needed companionship and helped me accept my validity in the world. He introduced me to his friendship circle, one of whom turned out to be a gym crush of mine. His name was Josh and he was an absolute Adonis. Josh and I ended up having a lengthy 'friends with benefits' situation over the next few months and I can't tell you how immensely that helped rebuild my self-esteem. When I first saw him at the gym, I had thought he was completely out of my league and would always just be that beautiful Greek statue of a man who I surreptitiously spied on in the gym mirrors ... and yet, within months, we were spending much of our weeks together. He was probably the most progressive person I had ever met. He was a free spirit who was also insanely kind and caring to anyone with whom he came in contact. It's sad that I needed to feel that recognition from someone like him in order to recognise my own worth, and sad to think that I needed to rely on a new friend in Ryan to pluck me out of my deep depression during that time – but I consider myself exceptionally lucky to have found such amazing friends during this difficult period.

It would also be remiss of me to not acknowledge a family member who was there for me throughout everything. My cousin Mary is a real-life Wonder Woman whose friendship and strength have been constant inspirations to me. She handles stress and adversity with a grace and ease that put me to shame and, for a long time during the teething period of my adjustment to this new life, she mothered me so well. We are the same age and had spent our early childhoods together. When she was a teenager, she moved in with my family so she could be educated in Sydney. She also went to Tangara School for Girls, the Opus Dei school that my mother had taught at, and was equally as miffed by the bizarre worldview that those schools were trying to encourage in the kids they were responsible for preparing for life. Unlike me, she never wallowed in self-pity but had taken life by the horns and has built herself into a business mogul and an ultra-mum. Before coming out to my dad and my sister, I had tested the waters with Mary first as I had always considered her more sister than cousin. She matter-of-factly stated that she had always known and didn't care. She followed that up by asking me to be her firstborn's godfather, which I am sure to this day has caused much debate within her own large family. Despite her responsibilities to her own family, as well as working thirty-four hours a day, she was never once not there for me. When I was at my lowest, she was there. When I was being self-indulgent in my situation, she hit me with hard truths. And every day, by merely witnessing her resilience, she continued to motivate me and spurred me further into adulthood. As embarrassing as it is to admit, I, a man in my mid-thirties, was still acting like a petulant child and she was the one who forced me to snap out of it and grow the fuck up.

When I had first moved back to Sydney in 2021, Mary opened her home up to me, as I had taken a job that wasn't far from where she lived. The night before my first shift at the new job, I was so caught up in my own 'woe is me' privileged self-indulgence that I decided to drown my sorrows in an entire bottle of vodka. I wandered the streets of her neighbourhood in a blackout drunken haze and returned to her house in the early hours of the morning. The doors had been locked, so I crawled in through the doggy door. A couple of hours later, she shook me awake as I was about to be late for work. I had vomited all over her guest-room bed. With her hands already more than full, she took care of everything and delivered me to work on time, though not without stern words of warning.

If there was anyone in the world who I had never wanted to be a burden on, it was her. With nothing but love in her heart, she took me to task for this behaviour, and her frank demeanour and our lifetime of friendship were the kick up my privileged backside that I needed. She gave me the strength to forge on ahead, and I'm sure she was delighted when she saw me making new friends and beginning to get myself together.

With the clouds starting to part after the disarray of the past few years, and with help and guidance from Mary and my new support system in Sydney, things began to fall into place. I was cast in a film called *Godless: The Eastfield Exorcism*. The script had been sent to me almost a year earlier, in August 2020, when I was still living with my dad and his wife. It was a film, based on a shocking true story, that centred on a married woman with mental health issues who had been misdiagnosed, by her religious husband, as being demonically possessed. She was then exposed to brutal abuse, all in the name of God, and I was cast as the zealous minister performing the exorcism. It was a dark and scary drama, and the character I was tasked to play reminded me of the exact type of person that I had always felt persecuted by. The opinionated people with absolute blind faith who didn't care about how their words and actions impacted the psyches of the vulnerable. Though I knew this world well, it also presented the biggest acting challenge I had faced to date.

This movie only came my way because of my dear friend and pseudo-brother, Dan Ewing. We had played siblings in the past and had remained strong friends over the years. The script had been sent to him as an offer to play the husband of the woman being exorcised. Another actor had been offered the role as the exorcist, but after Dan had read the script he called the director and urged for me to be cast instead. Dan knew everything about my struggles. He understood me and he knew when he read this script that I suited the role by virtue of the fact that I had lived within that world of religious zealotry. I had come out to him while we were playing brothers on *Red Billabong* and he had always been so encouraging. We quickly developed a brotherly relationship, and he's one of the few people I know who I have always felt completely seen by.

I filmed an audition scene from the film at my friend Jordan Rodrigues' Sydney apartment. Thom Green, also of

Dance Academy fame, joined us. It was a seven-page monologue of my character performing a religious exorcism, spouting Bible verses and using them against the poor woman. We workshopped it for a few hours. I channelled the teachers I had been educated by, and even some of the classmates who had destroyed my self-worth. It was the most truthful and vulnerable audition I had ever done, and it was great that I had the chance to unwind with some of my best mates afterward as I was very rattled by the whole thing. Though the rolling lockdowns had halted production of the film multiple times, it suddenly resurfaced at the exact moment that I had decided to shake everything off and open myself up to future possibilities.

I was cast and flew to Melbourne to spend a week in rehearsals with my co-stars, workshopping the intense scenes we would be filming together. A few weeks later, I was on set in a remote part of country Victoria.

The thing that struck me most about the script, and the story it was based on, was how voiceless the victim was. She was a woman who just needed mental health care, and yet the people she loved and trusted the most in life had determined that she was possessed by the devil. No matter how hard she fought against their beliefs, her voice didn't matter and she was subjected to brutal treatment. I couldn't help but draw comparisons to my own upbringing, with the community's blindness to the real issues at play and always using 'religion' to save the day. Though, as a person, I identified more with the female protagonist of the film, I had known people like my character my entire life. But, despite that, it felt almost too close to home and I was terrified that I wouldn't be able to deliver on my performance. I plugged myself into the mindset I had had for so many years, and I drew inspiration from the people I had grown up with.

Though I love to act, and I get tremendous fulfilment from being part of a creative process, it was a tough shoot. It required a lot from me to play that level of pig-headed zealotry after I had spent so many years trying to get away from it. And apart from all of that, I needed to be incredibly nasty each and every day on set in order to play my character correctly. There was also a complicated feeling for me, personally, that I was somewhat betraying my roots by portraying a religious character in such a negative light. And yet, not only was this a true story, but I had suffered at the hands of these ideologies myself and knew that there was no lie in the story we were telling. So, despite fears that I wouldn't be able to fulfil the role requirements, because my imposter syndrome was screaming at me that I wasn't good enough of an actor to play this part, I grabbed the role by the horns and found myself in the wilting Victorian summer heat, inside a sweltering tin shed, inflicting extreme acts of religious fanaticism on an innocent victim. Obviously, just pretend for the cameras.

In actual fact, that film shoot was the most rewarding professional experience I had had. Not only was it a booster shot in a career that had lain dormant for years, but it was the biggest acting challenge I had ever faced, and came at a time when I desperately needed to prove myself to myself.

Josh came and stayed with me for a time on that shoot. It was a new feeling to 'go to work', which required me to access the darkest recesses of my religious beliefs and perform horrible acts to someone, and then return home to a cooked meal, a bathtub surrounded by lit candles and a kiss from a handsome man. My acting career had always been so separate from my personal life, so it was nice to be able to have the two at once and have a break from the insane and nasty things I was required to do each day while working.

One day, I went to the local pub in the small village we were filming at and joined the crew for drinks. I walked in as my gay self. The crew had only ever seen me in character as an evil religious zealot. It was funny to see how shocked they all were when I arrived without any of the trappings of the character they saw me as. But I can't lie: it was also a huge boost of confidence to know that I must have been playing the character so well that they had no idea I was such an unmitigated fairy!

When we completed the film, even though I had played a character who was very much in line with how I had been raised, I felt the biggest sense of accomplishment that I had ever felt as an actor. Regardless of where this film went, I knew that I had dug deep and given it my all. It is rare to feel, as an actor, that you are on the same page with the creative team behind the project, and yet we all had a shared vision for the film and everyone on that set gave their utmost in order to achieve it. It is my proudest accomplishment to date, and I will forever hold a place in my heart for the beautiful film that we managed to create together under the most difficult of circumstances.

At the end of the shoot, I found a new apartment in Sydney and made a concerted effort to continue to build on the confidence that I was starting to feel. Unfortunately for me, I was starting to realise that my feelings for Josh were growing beyond the 'friends with benefits' thing we had going on, but I knew where he stood and it would be unfair of me to expect anything more when we had always been so clear about what our relationship was. I decided to bow out gracefully, and slowly distance myself so that things wouldn't get weird.

He did, however, take me to my first ever Mardi Gras in 2022. I was entering my late thirties and had never once experienced the famous Sydney Gay and Lesbian Mardi Gras. It was my first time truly enjoying and experiencing the love and acceptance of the queer community, surrounded by people who had overcome similar obstacles in their lives in the pursuit of their own authenticity. Pride suddenly made sense to me and, seeing so many people sharing their joy in life with one another, I realised how senseless it was to have been so caught up my whole life by the opinions of a small few.

Emboldened by this new lease on life, I felt confident enough to start putting myself out there for real. I wasn't a huge fan of hook-up culture – though I did dabble, I won't lie. As I had always been a relationship guy and with age not exactly being on my side, I wanted to find someone I could share my life with. I started going on proper dates and finally started to understand what I was really looking for in a partner, and what I actually brought to the table without any pretence about who I was.

This was when I started to encounter the 'fourteen-day itch', as I call it. Even though I was pushing thirty-seven, I was new to the scene. Though I did meet a few people and went out on many dates, I started to notice that after about two weeks, the other person's interest would suddenly wane and they'd want to move on. It was obviously not pleasant to witness this, but it was also part of that rite of passage that I had been wanting and I think it was necessary for me to experience that. You have to take the bad with the good.

However, over time, I began experiencing some significant side effects from being a single man in Sydney. Though the two-week relationships had all been fun, I started to feel like there was something unlikeable about me because I couldn't keep someone's attention in the way that they had mine. I dated a lovely British boy who seemed so eager at first and then, around the two-week mark, suddenly stopped replying to me. I met a gorgeous Danish boy who would come around in the morning with coffees and pastries only to then completely ignore my existence. I developed a crush on a guy I was working with who, as soon as he kissed me, decided he wanted to have nothing to do with me. I was asked out by an incredibly handsome and charming European man who I was so smitten by that I took the risk of asking him to be my date to a red-carpet event. It was the first time I had ever done a red carpet with a man, but I received a text from him afterward telling me that he only viewed us as friends.

It kept happening over and over again. I realised that though I had daydreamed of this single life, I actually hated it. I had considered myself brave for trying to date again and yet, at every turn, I was only ever feeling rejection. Old insecurities returned, and I started to feel like I would never find love again.

One night, I felt particularly miserable. I didn't want to overstretch the friendships I had made recently, as I had driven some friends away in the past by oversharing. So I tried to call my sister, who I had been making an effort to reconnect with since returning to Australia. It was somewhat unfair of me to expect that she would drop everything for me, and yet I remembered the example that my mother had set, and I knew that, no matter what, Mum would have done just that. Perhaps it was completely unfair of me to ask it, but I wanted to feel the same level of love and support from my family that my sister had received and been taught to provide. She, however, declined. It was clear that her reason for not being there for me in that moment was still due more to my sexuality than to anything else. With a hefty sigh, she told me, 'Tim, you know how I feel about all this.'

So I pivoted and talked to a friend from school. Like me, he had come out after we had left Redfield. However, unlike me, he seemed to have found a healthy balance between that conservative world and his ability to live his own life. I shared with him how miserable I was and how futile everything was feeling.

Unbeknownst to me, he shared what I was saying with a school group chat. He was well-intentioned, asking for people to pray for me because I was in a bad way. But one of my former classmates, who had become an Opus Dei numerary while he was still a teenage student, then contacted me. He had never been one of the bullies and was truly a good person. He called me because he was concerned about me and wanted to drive over to see me and, in his words, 'pray with me'. Though there had never been any friction between us, I told him that I didn't feel he would have anything to offer me as I knew the biases that were behind his apparent *act of kindness*. I insisted that he not make the effort.

Instead, I called Josh. We were very much just friends at this point but, being the kind person that he was, he suggested we get dinner together and watch a movie. As he made his way over to my place, I took a nap. I was awoken by Josh buzzing my apartment. I let him up and was about to take a shower so we could go about our plans when my buzzer rang again.

Josh and I were greeted at my apartment door by a host of police officers and ambulance crews. Despite me telling the numerary schoolmate to not bother coming to see me, he had done so regardless. When he had arrived at my apartment, he hadn't known which number was mine and had tried to call me. I had been napping, so I had simply missed his calls. He then took it upon himself to call emergency services, concerned that I was taking my own life.

I was sectioned under the *Mental Health Act*, handcuffed by the cops and placed in an ambulance. Amid the chaos, the numerary who had made the call was standing with the police and constantly reminding me how much God loved me. I told him to never talk to me again. I was taken to a local hospital and placed in a psychiatric ward until I could be assessed by a psychiatrist. It didn't matter to the police or ambulance staff that I had a friend with me and that we had perfectly normal plans for the evening. Josh stayed with me the whole time. He crawled up in the small hospital bed with me and didn't leave my side throughout the entire ordeal.

After about sixteen hours in the psych ward, I was eventually interviewed by the psychiatrist, who also spoke at length with Josh. It was determined that the whole thing was just a misunderstanding, and yet the events that had transpired did more damage than good. I couldn't have felt worse about myself after I was released. The next evening, I was legitimately suicidal as a consequence, and had myself sectioned in the psych ward again.

It took a long time to get over that experience. As much of a shock to the system as it had been, it was mostly a wake-up call. The past few years had proven the benefits of letting go, and so I realised it was time to once and for all let go of my sister. My unrealistic expectations of our family bond were at the root of all the drama, and it was only by holding onto hope that I continually felt so let down by her. It was obvious now that it would be better and more peaceful for us both if I just left our relationship where it was and stopped hoping. I also had to be honest with myself. Yes, I had been lonely, but I had been wallowing in it. It was time to grow up and sort myself out. I decided I wasn't going to seek love out anymore. I would wait for it to find me. I stopped trying to meet people online, where filtered photos and the Instagram era of false perfection were rampant. Instead, I wanted a good old-fashioned meet-cute from the movies, where boy meets boy unexpectedly and romance gets a chance to blossom outside the contrivances of modern dating expectations. I just needed to be patient and wait. And as clichéd as it sounds, I needed to find happiness within myself. 'No boys for at least six months,' I vowed to myself.

The world really does move in mysterious ways. Only a month or so after my experience in the psych ward, I was contacted by investigative journalist Louise Milligan, who was putting together a documentary about the school system that I was raised in, its connections with Opus Dei and its reach within the political sphere. By then, a fellow student from Redfield College, Dominic Perrottet, whose parents had both been Opus Dei supernumeraries, had become the premier of New South Wales and was seeking re-election. Louise was putting together a report that detailed the archaic teachings that the school system had been forcing vulnerable children into believing for decades. Her report had been cooking for some time when she called to see if I would be interested in taking part. After my recent run-in with my former school friend, the timing felt significant. I had never had a voice when I had been confined within the walls of the school, but now I had a platform to say my piece. So I accepted her proposal.

I was terrified by the idea. Even though I had come to the conclusion that my upbringing had worked very hard against me in my endeavours as an adult, I had really only *just* come to that conclusion. But the timing felt fortuitous. It struck me that this could be an opportunity to speak out on behalf of others who had gone through similar experiences, not just within Opus Dei but in the blind world of long-held beliefs. As someone who had gone through the meat grinder and come out the other side with a sense that my issues had never been caused by my sexuality but rather by the opinions of the people around me, I knew firsthand just how voiceless the victims of this kind of rhetoric felt. Sharing my experiences in such a public forum could perhaps make some sort of change in the world.

I didn't really want to do it, but my recent experiences had shown that, although twenty years had passed since my time at Redfield College, the same attitudes and behaviours still existed. It felt like I had a responsibility to share what I could.

I didn't want my participation to come across as any kind of retaliation, so I wasn't interested in making any outrageous allegations. I was going to talk honestly about my experiences and keep it at that. It was nerve-racking, but I trusted that it was the right thing to do.

On the rare occasions that I had a chance to speak with my sister over the years, before we completely stopped talking, she had often implied that I was being selfish for simply seeking out the same happiness and fulfilment that she was privileged enough to always take for granted due to her heterosexuality. She continued over the years to encourage me to seek help from the conversion support group she had linked me to, and when I had categorically told her that it would not change a damn thing, she had said that I needed to be more charitable, stop thinking about myself and do something for others. While I'm sure her intention wasn't for me to denounce the education system and religious community we had grown up in as a charitable act, I put her advice into play and decided that I could do more good by telling my own story. That way, I could stand up for the kids who were being subjected to the exact same treatment that I had endured during my formative years.

Then, out of nowhere, as I was busy fretting about shooting the upcoming report, I got my meet cute. I had been working as a gym manager and started to get attention from one of our regular members. One evening while I was at work, he made a flirtatious comment to me.

I'd like to think of myself as glib, but only gibberish came out of my mouth in response. I was mortified afterward, wishing the ground would swallow me up whole. He thought my embarrassment was cute and was undeterred. We would bump into each other at random intervals over the next few months, always with the same awkward tension between us but never anything more. Then, one night, he mentioned that he would like to have my number. As unprofessional as it felt, I scribbled it down on a Post-it note, only to find that he had already walked away. I gave it to him a few days later when I saw him next, though I decided not to put any pressure on it. It would be up to him if he wanted to follow through or not.

A week later, I showed up, typically late, to our first date. As the car turned the corner, I saw him standing there with a big bouquet of flowers. I started to fret immediately. *Was I ready for this? Would he, too, get bored of me in a week? Was I opening myself up to get hurt again?* However, the date went spectacularly. He was so smart and had such a kind demeanour. He made no assumptions and it was clear that we were only getting to know each other. I found him fascinating and our two energies seemed to complement each other. We sat in a cute rooftop bar with the Sydney skyline as our backdrop and the hours flew by while we chatted. As the sun started to set, bathing us in an orange-pink glow, he politely asked me if he could kiss me. I have to say, it was very romantic and an absolute cracker of a first date, but I still wasn't convinced that I was ready to give this whole dating thing another shot yet. However, after ghosting him for a week while I tried to figure it all out, I felt compelled to ask him out a second time.

I'm really glad I did. We have been together ever since, and none of the toxicity or people-pleasing that had led me astray in the past has ever been part of our relationship. He has been patient and supportive in my efforts to move past the PTSD from my previous relationships. Our ability to work through things constructively and lovingly is like nothing I have ever experienced. We started dating just a few weeks before I was going to be interviewed by Louise Milligan for the *Four Corners* documentary about Opus Dei and my school. He understood the gravity of what I was doing and supported me every step along the way.

It was as the new year ticked over that I realised I had found the comfort in myself I had been longing for all my life. It might have taken thirty-seven years, but it was nice to have finally arrived. Though I was quietly shitting myself about the imminent release of the documentary and the potential shockwaves it would send through my family and the Opus Dei community, I felt emboldened by the risk. And I felt brave, and I felt proud.

CHAPTER FOURTEEN

Vocation

The *Four Corners* episode, 'Purity: An Education in Opus Dei', aired on 30 January 2023. It detailed the Pared schools' intricate ties with the secretive Opus Dei sect and how the archaic views of the organisation shaped the education being provided. Not only did the episode showcase some of the damaging, ignorant and irresponsible ideals being spread among the students in their care, but it also delved into the structure of the Opus Dei organisation and how the schools were being used to mould kids to their own small-world views while withholding the real world around them.

The documentary aired almost ten years to the day since that night in the LA gay sports bar where I had whispered to Sam that I'd had a crush on him and finally experienced my first proper kiss. Despite the decade in between, I hadn't said anything publicly about my sexuality. I had alluded to it once or twice on my socials, but I hadn't ever wanted to make a huge announcement of it. I figured that one day it would just get picked up on and I'd say, 'Yeah, I'm gay,' and not make it a big deal, since it never should have been one in the first place.

It would also somehow feel tacky if I made a whole song and dance about it. So the documentary ended up being my outing, though it was pipped at the post by a tabloid magazine that ran a story about me being gay a day before the documentary aired.

In the documentary, I spoke of the homophobia within the Opus Dei/Pared community, and of the claustrophobic world created by their constant monitoring. I talked about the isolation felt by the queer students there, and how damaging and long-term the effects are of the bullying received from fellow students, which the schools turn a blind eye to.

It was an intensely surreal experience to watch it as it aired. I had joined a few other ex-students from my school who had also been gay boys studying around the same time as myself and had received the same treatment. It was very odd to reflect on the fact that, only ten years earlier, I had been living in such fear of myself that I couldn't even say the words 'I'm gay' while coming out to Alicia – and yet now I was on national television sharing my biggest secret and calling for an end to bigoted homophobia. It was even more surreal to think of the guy I had been years before then, when I would sit in church for twenty minutes past the end of mass, praying for God to take the gay away. And yet he didn't.

Instead, God gave me a unique life with unique experiences that had all led directly to this moment. That vocation Mum had spoken so much about – that thing each of us is individually called to do with our lives in service of others – maybe this was it. She had obviously intended me for the priesthood, the idea of which had always filled me with dread and despair. But suddenly becoming a voice speaking out on behalf of the LGBTQI+ community felt far more right. It was genuine and important.

I had no way of anticipating the response to the episode, but I was terrified of my family's reaction. My dad and his wife were ashamed that I had done it, though they admitted that they hadn't actually watched the program. And I heard a rumour that my sister was telling people in her conservative bubble that a restraining order had been put out against me, which is false. This reception was somewhat expected, however.

But then, a few months after the episode aired, my grandmother passed away, and I wasn't told or invited to the funeral. This was my mother's mum. The same grandmother who had been a huge part of my life. Though she had forty grandchildren, I was the most involved in her life and had spent years taking care of her while simultaneously caring for my mother. She died one month shy of her 101st birthday. I received a text message from a cousin innocently asking why I wasn't at the funeral. That was how I found out she had passed away. Perhaps I hadn't been told because the family were purposefully trying to ostracise me after the documentary. The other option was that I had simply been forgotten. I'm not sure which is worse.

But though that did sting, what resonated far stronger were the positive reactions. Within minutes of the program finishing, I was inundated by messages. While it was incredibly affirming to have so many people reach out with nice things to say, what really touched me to my core were the people from all across the world, strangers who I had never met, sending me their own similar stories and thanking me for speaking on their behalf. Stuck in their own cages, they hadn't realised that they were not alone and that they needed their voices to be heard.

I have always felt such tremendous fulfilment from making movies and TV series. I love being part of the entertainment industry and making a positive impact on people's days by providing them with distraction or escapism. And being lucky enough to have been part of some truly special projects with incredible fan bases, I have seen how much joy they have brought to so many people. But this was a different feeling.

This felt like an honour, and it felt noble. My time had come and gone. I had travelled through the fire and gotten out on the other side. There was nothing for me to personally gain from speaking up other than my knowledge that what I had to say could go a long way toward ending the suffering of others. Reading hundreds of firsthand accounts, from people who were feeling exactly as I had for such a long time, confirmed the very real importance of what I had just taken part in, and what more I could potentially do.

I had spent years struggling to find my feet, but now everything started falling into place. A few months after the documentary aired, my film *Godless: The Eastfield Exorcism* had its world premiere in New Orleans. I attended with the rest of the cast and couldn't help but recognise the irony in me playing a religious zealot whose blind faith resulted in the death of a voiceless victim, while at the same time making a name for myself as someone speaking out against religious zealotry. This premiere also finally provided me with an opportunity to return to America.

After so many years feeling like the pandemic had taken me away from my life over there and yearning to return, I was back. I took the opportunity to make a quick pit stop to LA. I had dearly missed my friends there, and had left a couple of suitcases worth of clothes behind in my old apartment. But what really intrigued me was seeing how the city would make me feel when I got back.

Depressed. That is how it made me feel. I was instantly reminded of all the stress and anxiety that had characterised my time there, and remembered just how incredibly lost I had felt living there. I had reached out to Ken to see if I could gather my belongings from him, but he declined to respond. That chapter of my life was well and truly over, and I was at peace with that fact. I could live without those clothes because I had gained something so much more valuable: self-respect, and comfort in who I was. I was only there for a couple of days and caught up with as many people as I could, revisiting our old favourite hangouts. It was cathartic to be able to recognise that LA no longer held the same lustre for me, and I was glad to let it go.

Shortly after getting back to Australia, I started work on a new film called *Body Blow*. A fast-paced film noir thriller, due for release in 2025, it was my first time in a gay role.

Portraying a gay character was yet another thing that I had vehemently vowed never to do, even after I came out. Yet now I was embracing it with excitement and enthusiasm. Though my casting in this film, the release of *Godless* and the airing of the documentary were all completely coincidental events, I saw a weird symbiosis in how everything was starting to shape up. I couldn't ignore the trajectory that I was on. The roars from the demons that had plagued me all my life had been reduced to whispers.

Over the next few months, I was contacted by various journalists who wanted me to share more of my stories and experiences, especially my exposure to conversion therapy practices. A new bill was being introduced before the parliament of New South Wales that would once and for all make conversion therapy illegal. I recalled a conversation I once had with my father, during a particularly heated family argument, when I had brought up my experience with the psychologist and stated that it was illegal in some states of Australia. His response to me had been, 'Not in *every* state,' like that excused it. I hold nothing against my father anymore these days, and I know his response was more of a kneejerk reaction, but those words rang in my ears when I was offered the opportunity to speak out against those practices.

In late 2023, Equality Australia, a non-profit organisation that champions the rights of the LGBTQI+ community, asked me to publicly share my experiences with the psychologist who tried to hypnotise the gay out of me when I was in my twenties. They wanted to highlight the need for conversion therapy practices to be definitively banned in the state of New South Wales. The resulting video from that conversation was later released. It felt good to use my experiences to contribute to the future in a meaningful way. My story received an overwhelmingly positive response, but it was also interesting to note some of the negative responses. Of course I had anticipated the handful of delightfully worded messages of hate, from accounts that disappeared almost as soon as the messages were sent – a heroic and brave move by the conservative keyboard mafia. But what really stuck with me was a common thread among some of the more middle-ground people – they weren't necessarily being hateful or aggressive in their language, but instead seemed confused as to why I had found myself in that position in the first place, given how old I was and the fact that I should have had more autonomy over the situation. Remarks like this one, from a Reddit user commenting on the video: 'It's actually quite a dumb story. He was 26 years old and was offered hypnotherapy for his homosexuality. I mean, just say no thank you? Is it really that hard to be an adult?'

The simplest answer to this is, yes, it really *was* that hard. Internalised homophobia had me in its clutches from an early age, and the circumstances surrounding my exposure to conversion practices were that I was coerced under false pretences – as would be the case for many others. I was once again happy to share my story to raise awareness about the psychological harm that conversion practices pose.

Over the next several months, I continued to work with Equality Australia as the bill got closer and closer to being introduced to parliament. Together with other survivors, I had a meeting with the new Premier of New South Wales, Chris Minns, and member of the Legislative Council, Penny Sharpe, to urge for the bill's introduction and support the efforts to provide protection for vulnerable people. A week later, the bill was introduced. We held a press conference at Parliament House and later spoke with members of Parliament about the importance of this bill.

In early 2024, the new Equality Bill passed the floor of Parliament and conversion therapy practices were finally banned in the state of New South Wales. I had no idea when I timidly accepted the invite to be part of Louise Milligan's documentary that, twelve months later, I would play a role in changing legislation. The teenage version of me, who wished with all his might that he would wake up as a different person and no longer have to suffer the burden of being himself, never would have imagined that one day he'd be a public advocate for LGBTQI+ equality. Yet here I am.

With that in mind, I do hope that anyone who has read this and needed to feel that they aren't alone can find some comfort in the stories I've shared. I hope that, though I've made no bones about how bumpy a ride it was, you know now that there is a life that you deserve waiting for you. And I hope that you never let go of the spark you have inside you, even if no-one else seems to see it. Hold on to it. It will get you through and it deserves your attention far more than the negative things that are being said around you. To quote the Redfield College school motto, 'Veritas Liberabit Vos.' *The truth will set you free.*

Being gay caused many problems for me during the developmental stages of my life and the scars run very deep. The demons will always be with me, but I have learned how to keep them at bay most of the time. I dearly wish I could still have a relationship with my sister, nieces and nephews. But I've learned that sometimes it's best to just walk away and be grateful for the memories. At the tender age of forty, I feel I took years to find my path in life, but I've learned that it's never too late to start searching.

Above all else, the main lesson I have learned from life is, ironically, that the truth does indeed set you free. Though 'Veritas Liberabit Vos' is Redfield's school motto, the way I was raised within their Opus Dei community turned my truth into a cage. It took years of setbacks, tears, suicidal moments and learning lessons in some of the hardest ways possible to get to where I am today. But I am proud to say that this *is* my truth, and I am finally free.

Acknowledgements

For at least fifteen years, people have been telling me I should write a book about my life. Back then, half of the events described in these pages hadn't yet happened, and I was still very much in the closet at the time. And yet, my life already resembled a far-fetched soap opera. It was my first indication that the normal I knew was actually far from it. These people planted the seeds and it was off the back of their years of encouragement that I finally took the plunge.

Specifically, I would like to thank my mates Dave, Russ, Dan and my cousin Mary, as well as my adopted *Dance Academy* family. They have all stayed by my side through tremendous years of transition and struggle. Their unwavering friendship gave me the resilience I needed during this process and their words of wisdom and support have made me the man I am today.

I owe a debt of gratitude to Claire Harris and Louise Milligan, who provided me with a platform to finally speak openly about my experiences. While it was daunting to come out publicly on national television, I was inspired by Louise's tireless efforts to stand up for people who can't stand up for themselves. It was the catalyst for a new purpose in my life. No longer was I trying to find my own voice, but I understood that sharing my experiences was lending a voice to others who are denied it.

Thanks also to Anna Brown and the wonderful people at Equality Australia who further empowered me in what I had to say. They gave me the ability to turn my negative experiences into the possibility for positive change. They have proven to me the power of resistance and it was with this new confidence that I felt ready to accept this opportunity.

However, this wouldn't have happened if it weren't for Scott Henderson, who first reached out to me about turning my story into a book. It is not lost on me how lucky I am that my first work as a writer is being published, and I am forever grateful.

I wouldn't have been able to get through this process, however, without the amazing Annie, Sophie and the entire team at Hachette, who held my hand throughout the process. As such a novice, I'm sure I caused them many a frustration. Together with the generous mentorship I received from Greg, Anthony Venn-Brown and Sacha Horler, their nurturing and advice has been invaluable.

And to my new friends, over the recent years: thank you for believing in me. Thank you for understanding why I've been such a hermit for the past eighteen months and for understanding the importance of what I am trying to do. You are the very definition of human kindness, and I'm so lucky to have you in my life.

Lastly, to my partner. I couldn't have done this without you. Your patient and kind understanding of what this project meant to me has been the one thing that has gotten me through it. The late nights, the weekly mental breakdowns, and the fact that you also gave up a year of your life so that I could complete this journey. Words will never do justice to how I feel, so I'll just show you. For the rest of our lives.

About the Author

Tim Pocock is an Australian actor, producer, musician and advocate originally from Johannesburg, South Africa. An award-winning pianist and singer, Tim began his career on the Sydney Opera House stage at a young age, before embarking on a successful career in the film and television industry. With credits including *X-Men Origins: Wolverine*, *Home and Away*, the multi-Logie-winning series *Dance Academy* and the three-time AACTA-nominated film *Godless: The Eastfield Exorcism*, for which he also served as executive producer, Tim also stars in the noir thriller *Body Blow*, set for release in 2025.

In recent years, Tim has set his sights on advocating for the LGBTQI+ community, speaking out on institutionalised homophobia and playing an active part in recent legislative changes made in the NSW Parliament's criminalisation of conversion therapy practices.